"It's often said our deepest spiritual awakenings follow tragedy, loss or some deep-rooted chaos that turns our world upside down when we least expect it. In A Soulful Awakening, the author shares her soul's journey with us in a beautifully written masterpiece documenting one woman's journey through adversity to enlightenment. This book will challenge you to look within, question your beliefs and the way you look at life. If you are open to the gifts within these pages, there just may be a special message waiting for you. Every now and then we run across a book that forever changes us, and this is that book for me. Thank you, Stephanie Banks, for a heartfelt and honest portrayal of an emerging soul so eloquently written."

—SHANDA TROFE,
Founder of the Spiritual Writers Network

"Stephanie's awakening after her accident, and the subsequent journey through her soul space, has opened channels offering us mystical insights and profound wisdom. Fellow travelers will be inspired and enlightened."

—LINDA MACKAY,
clinical therapist, yoga and meditation practitioner

Damien

Who would have thought I would write a Book! Actually... I have known this since a kid "your intuition is the Blueprint to your lifetime Masterpiece"

A Soulful Awakening

One woman's extraordinary journey from life to death to a soulful awakening

STEPHANIE BANKS

BALBOA.
PRESS
A DIVISION OF HAY HOUSE

Copyright © 2014 Stephanie Banks.

All rights reserved. No part of this book may be used or reproduced by any means, graphic, electronic, or mechanical, including photocopying, recording, taping or by any information storage retrieval system without the written permission of the publisher except in the case of brief quotations embodied in critical articles and reviews.

Balboa Press books may be ordered through booksellers or by contacting:

Balboa Press
A Division of Hay House
1663 Liberty Drive
Bloomington, IN 47403
www.balboapress.com
1 (877) 407-4847

Because of the dynamic nature of the Internet, any web addresses or links contained in this book may have changed since publication and may no longer be valid. The views expressed in this work are solely those of the author and do not necessarily reflect the views of the publisher, and the publisher hereby disclaims any responsibility for them.

The author of this book does not dispense medical advice or prescribe the use of any technique as a form of treatment for physical, emotional, or medical problems without the advice of a physician, either directly or indirectly. The intent of the author is only to offer information of a general nature to help you in your quest for emotional and spiritual well-being. In the event you use any of the information in this book for yourself, which is your constitutional right, the author and the publisher assume no responsibility for your actions.

Any people depicted in stock imagery provided by Thinkstock are models, and such images are being used for illustrative purposes only. Certain stock imagery © Thinkstock.

Printed in the United States of America.

ISBN: 978-1-4525-2032-2 (sc)
ISBN: 978-1-4525-2034-6 (hc)
ISBN: 978-1-4525-2033-9 (e)

Library of Congress Control Number: 2014914707

Balboa Press rev. date: 08/29/2014

Acknowledgments

Thank you seems like an inadequate phrase to describe my gratitude to all those who continue to guide and teach us as we travel through this journey of life. On behalf of all those who benefit from this book, I say thank you to all our physical and non-physical guides, teachers, and protectors for all your profound insight and love.

Contents

Letter to the Reader ix
Introduction xiii

Chapter 1: The Bike Crash 1
Chapter 2: Awakening to Our Non-physical Realm 6
Chapter 3: Brushing Cheek-to-Cheek with Death 16
Chapter 4: The Magic of Synchronicities 27
Chapter 5: Life at Grenville 37
Chapter 6: The Beginning of the End 44
Chapter 7: Hello and Good-bye 56
Chapter 8: Denial and Acceptance 62
Chapter 9: Bonnie's Story 82
Chapter 10: The Evangelist 89
Chapter 11: We Are All One 98
Chapter 12: Times Are Changing 106

Conclusion 113
Affirmations and Poems 119
Channeled Definitions 125
About the Author 131

Letter to the Reader

"What you seek is seeking you."
—Rumi

Dear Reader,

I would like to begin by saying thank you. Thank you for awakening to your higher self and allowing your intuition to guide you to this book. This book comes to you as a result of a mountain biking crash in August of 2012. For a brief moment, I died, spent time with my guardian Ruby, and with a renewed sense of my life's purpose, returned to my broken body with no immediate memory of my experience. My injuries forced me to sit still, and as I sat in my oversized chair, which I fondly refer to as my eagle's nest, I began to put words to the pages of an empty journal. I quickly realized that these words were coming from a non-physical realm where our lost loved ones, spirit guides, teachers and protectors reside.

As time passed and my confidence in the messages I was receiving increased, I began reading what I had transcribed to close friends and family. Eventually friends of friends, acquaintances, and people I had never met began requesting messages of their own. At first, I felt doubt and fear, but then I consciously returned to my roots that run deep into this vast universe and chose to openly share my newfound connection to our non-physical plane.

A year later and five journals full, I realized that the passages I had written were gifts for us all—gifts of profound wisdom and knowing delivered from a higher source of love and compassion. These messages are meant to be shared.

Those passages and messages transformed many lives right before my eyes, and this I could not ignore. Like never before, I realized the power and potential of what we are able to hear, feel, and experience when we simply allow ourselves the freedom to be still and open to all that surrounds us.

As I witnessed lives changing in such profound and positive ways, I knew this book needed to be available to all. It has been two years in the making and would not have been possible without the persistence, belief, and diligence of my life partner and the patience of our son. Together we sorted and compiled the best of the best—the cream of the crop, so to speak—of what had transpired within my journals. The messages themselves have not been edited, as I am merely a transmitter, and now you, as the reader and receiver, have become the translator. This book is here for you to explore and relate to in your own personal way. It is a tool, a guidebook to spark a soulful awakening and renewed awareness in each and every one of you.

As humans, we have an innate ability to learn through and with each other; therefore, I have included numerous accounts of my own personal experiences in life. At the end of each story, I have chosen messages from our non-physical guides and teachers that correlate and correspond in such a way that learning and growth from these experiences become possible. As you engage in these stories and lessons, I encourage you to look for similarities and common ground as they relate to your own personal life's journey. We all experience the same emotional turbulence and misguided priorities as we venture down our individual paths. Our experiences and how we choose to respond or react to these situations may differ, but the underlying lessons in all situations are the same. These lessons are quite simple as long as you keep them simple. Every experience in life, no matter how insignificant it may seem, is an opportunity for growth. Small, everyday changes lead to exponential growth on all levels.

Please accept this book as a gift that you deserve. Share this gift as you will, not with the expectation to change others but rather because you believe in the wisdom or peace that you have found within these messages. As others read and contemplate, they will translate the words in their own manner and may or may not choose to apply them to their own lives.

Introduction

"Turn your wounds into wisdom."
—Oprah

It's 8:00 a.m., snowy and beautiful outside. Here I sit in my big round chair situated in our round home, which is so conveniently placed on this round planet, known to me as an education center for the soul. As I sit here and contemplate an introduction for this book, I cannot help but take pause and feel completely humbled by the magnificence of our universe and all that it encompasses.

How is it possible that until August of 2012, I existed on such a shallow level of consciousness? Although I have always regarded myself as somewhat intuitive, compassionate, and loving, I recognize now that my potential was far greater than I had realized. The same is true for you, who are about to embark on this journey of self-reflection and self-discovery within these pages.

There is so much more to discover, experience, unleash, learn, share, and live. As you delve into these lessons and messages, feel the energy that surrounds their words, feel the beauty of the language that has so eloquently been delivered to us from our nonphysical guides, teachers, and protectors that exist in the realms that surround and engulf our own.

I am just as special as you; therefore, if I am able to hear and feel these words, then so, too, are you. Try to refrain from simply reading, and allow yourself to float through the messages as though they were written especially for you, because they were.

The words delivered are a reflection of our natural self. The messages are a gentle but firm reminder of who we are as opposed to who we have become through the adaptation of societal laws and expectations.

We are not here on earth to serve society, the economy, or our fears and emotional turmoil that are created as a result. We are here to learn all there is to learn about our higher being—our soul. We are here collectively for the same purpose of enlightenment and ascension.

As individuals and as a whole, we have strayed from our roots and have adopted habitual reactions from our foe: fear. We have a false belief that these reactions are aiding in our survival, but in true, unobstructed reality, we are strangling our spirits in this manner. These reactions, which are directed by a fear-based ego, encompass judgment, greed, resentment, narcissism, control, manipulation, and anger.

Fear is a misrepresentation of who we really are; it is a misguided source struggling for breath. It thrives upon our weak moments like a predator does with its prey. It creates darkness within us that prohibits learning within to transpire.

It is time to extinguish fear with love—love for ourselves and for all other fellow souls who share our wondrous universe. There is magic and mysticism within our world and the worlds that float freely around our own that is waiting to be recognized and acknowledged. Look for the beauty that emanates from all aspects of your life as you choose to engage on this journey of self-discovery. The peace that will enter your heart, your soul, will transform your outlook on life as you shed your layers of fear and reveal your core.

This is a love story between you and the universe. Like all love stories, there may be tragic times and moments that are trying, but those are the times when opportunity for growth is at its prime. Look for the courage that resides within you to find resilience, compassion, and trust when these times come upon you.

We are all born from the same source, live through the same source, and return to the same source. This entity is an entity of your own creation. As we individually create our own existence, we collectively create a universal existence. When we choose to create compassion individually, we choose to contribute compassion on a universal level.

We are all connected at our roots—individually bound to one another for eternity. This is something that we cannot change, and really, why would we want to? Allow what you learn while reading these messages from the universe to penetrate your core and your entire spirit—your soul. Your soul is your true being, your higher level of existence. It is the home to your heart. Your soul is where goodness resides and is craving to be discovered and nurtured.

I promise you that when you open your heart and allow the words of love to enter, your life will take on a whole new meaning. Fewer than seven months ago, I sat where many of you sit at the table of spiritual growth. I, too, existed in a reality that seemed to be distracted, directed, and dictated by money, power, and greed. I resided in a world that seemed foreign to me on a deeper level, but I had become so accustomed to this way of life that I did not know how to strive for change within myself.

I may have continued to keep rolling through life in this mundane fashion—carried on through my journey of life unaware of all that was so close to me but yet so far away—had certain circumstances not transpired on a balmy summer day while on a family vacation.

Chapter 1

The Bike Crash

"If opportunity doesn't knock, build a door."
—Milton Berie

Living an active outdoor life in British Columbia, Canada, at times brings with it certain consequences. For me, the consequences were a mountain-biking accident, which has brought this book to you.

Every August, Whistler, BC, Canada, is host to Crankworx weekend, where serious mountain bikers gather to test their courage, determination, and skill as they soar through the air and ride down the treacherous terrain that only expert mountain bikers dare to venture.

Neither my partner, Steve, nor I are hard-core downhill bikers, but we have ridden our share of cross-country trails with our son, Dawson. We decided as a family to take a three-day vacation to Whistler to test our own skill and partake in the Crankworx events from the perspective of spectators.

Stephanie Banks

Our weekend began with following a trail map to a few entry-level cross-country loops that we all enjoyed, yet felt that we could handle a little more of a challenge. Day two consisted of biking more intermediate technical trails and watching the world-class mountain bikers "huck their meat," as they say, over gigantic jumps created for this event. The plan for our last day was to tackle the ski hill on our bikes. As avid snowboarders, we are accustomed to ascending mountains on a chairlift or gondola and descending with snow beneath our boards, but we were not so accustomed to riding down a mountain on a bike. I was excited yet tentative at the same time.

On day three, the village of Whistler was swarming with people and pedals as we rolled our bikes toward the chairlift. Our bodies were shackled in safety gear, including full-face helmets. I had purchased mine on day one after following a step-by-step instructional guide to properly fitting and buying a mountain bike helmet. I had synchronistically found the how-to article in a magazine that I had purchased on a hunch at a gas station en route.

We loaded the chair along with our bikes that hung precariously on the outside. We started with a beginner run, but we all agreed to bump it up a notch and go to the next level. After successfully completing our first intermediate run, we were pumped with energy and adrenaline. As we rode the chair for the third time, we discussed the previous trail. We decided that we were all capable of managing ourselves skillfully on that particular run. The boys had discovered a jump they wanted to try, so we opted to do it again. We decided that when we got to the jump section, I would ride down first, bypass the jumps, stop at the bottom, and take pictures of Steve and Dawson jumping.

Once we arrived at this section, we waited for a few minutes, as there was a constant stream of riders. The blue run that we were riding intersected with a double-black diamond, an advanced run. From there, there were a series of jumps to choose from before continuing down the chosen trail.

For those of us who prefer to keep our feet and our wheels firmly planted on the ground, there was an alternate route around the jumps. This was where I had planned to go; however, something came over me at the last second, and I diverted from the alternate route, assuming that I could simply roll over one of the jumps without leaving the ground. I assumed that the jump I hastily decided to roll over was a tabletop, meaning that the launchpad and the transitioned landing were connected. But I failed to realize that there was an eight-foot gap between them with a rock gully beneath.

As I gained speed heading toward the jump, I briefly thought about stopping on the top to take a picture. But by the time I realized I wouldn't be stopping on the top because the top didn't exist, I felt my body and bike lift effortlessly from the ground and soar toward the rock face that lay in my path. I had almost gained enough momentum for my front tire to grab the top of the other side, but instead, my bike smashed forcefully into the rock wall, slamming my wrists into my handlebars while my full-face helmet bounced off the rock face.

I later learned that I had died upon impact. My heart stopped briefly as trauma built up and created blockages. But as quickly as my heart had stopped, it resumed again as my soul made the final decision to return to my life on earth—but with a renewed sense of self. I chose to hold conscious thought and intent in my heart in such a way that it would drive my existence here on earth. I returned to my body as though my death did not occur, as I did not have any recollection of the experience.

Stephanie Banks

When I collided with the rock wall, my eyes must have been wide-open, because I remember the beautiful lines that ran through the rock as I witnessed them up close. I felt my right pedal insert itself into my shin in the small gap between my pads, but oddly, I didn't feel any pain. As I fell backward into the crevasse below with my bike landing on top of me, I knew I was hurt.

During those few, brief moments when I smashed into the rock face and lay in a heap in the gully, I experienced no pain of any kind. It was as though someone had absorbed the pain for me, at least for a short time. That enabled me to see myself from a different perspective. I felt as though my body was separate from my core, as I knew I had made an error in judgment that would have repercussions.

As I lay on my back on the rocks in the gully, I saw another biker fly over me, unaware of my broken body below. Steve and Dawson, with the assistance of a kind German fellow who had witnessed the crash, diverted traffic from the gully section and made their way down the hill to assist me.

Patience has always been a challenge for me, so without hesitation, I began pulling my body to the top of the ledge. I vaguely recall scrambling my way out, and in hindsight, am uncertain how I managed. With the help of the boys, I found myself seated on a hillside, just off the track with my bike at my feet. I remember Steve discussing calling patrol, but I began to feel shock setting in; so without further contemplation, I hopped on my bike as though nothing had happened and proceeded to ride down the last half of the trail. Every twist, turn, root, and rock ricocheted through my body, creating excruciating pain, so I rode faster.

Steve later informed me that he had a difficult time keeping up with me as he followed my whimpers to the bottom. All I was able to focus on at the time was getting to the bottom and off my bike. It amazes me what humans are capable of accomplishing when in a state of panic or shock.

The journey seemed endless, like a dream. Finally, my eyes focused in on the village as I approached the final leg. Conveniently, there was a first-aid station at the bottom of the run that was set up for the weekend. After a brief assessment, I was shuttled to the hospital, where I emerged with a cast on each arm, whiplash, a bruised femur, numerous minor injuries, and the helmet that had saved my life.

Chapter 2

Awakening to Our Non-physical Realm

"Just as a candle cannot burn without fire, we cannot live without a spiritual life."
—Buddah

As we drove home from Whistler, my mind began racing down the track of worry and regret. I had responsibilities to my work, my son, my husband, and our small hobby farm. My brother and I were in the height of our season with multiple landscape projects on the go. As a hands-on business owner, I felt fearful of how my disabilities would impact our company.

Halfway home, I began to panic and found myself tearing at my right cast with my teeth. I had anticipated this when I sat before the doctor in the casting room at the hospital. I insisted that I would not be able to function independently with two casts, so I begged him to cut one of them open and then hold it together with a tensor bandage. The doctor reluctantly honored my wishes by choosing the wrist with the least damage and gave me strict instructions to take it easy if I chose to remove it at any time.

A Soulful Awakening

Steve stopped the vehicle and gently removed the cast from my right arm. He was much more successful than my teeth had been. With my right arm sore but free, I felt a moment of hope, and my horizons expanded as I held onto that feeling. I was thankful to be right-handed and would at least be able to brush my teeth, possibly drive an automatic work truck, and write.

The next two months of rehab were long and difficult, but I managed to deal with the pain without the assistance of medication and was faced with reestablishing a relationship with patience. I am an active, busy, independent fire sign who had yet to learn the art of sitting still. I believed that a successful person was a busy person.

The first two weeks were especially trying, as my family insisted that I stay home and recover. Although my right hand was free to move, I still had ample pain elsewhere in my body and felt imprisoned by my own physical restrictions. We live on a small farm away from anyone or anything, so I struggled with what to do with my time. I paced around the house and back and forth across our deck, grimacing in pain while fighting agitation and boredom. I tried reading, but my attention was short, as my mind would take over, opening the gates to anger and anguish. I would begin to pace once again. I quickly discovered that pacing back and forth across my deck did not contribute in a constructive manner to my mental or physical well-being.

Throughout my life, I have gone through periods when writing brought me solitude and peace. On one of my countless trips across my deck, I remembered this tried-and-true pastime. As though in a panic, I rummaged through my dresser looking for an empty journal I had purchased a few years prior at a fundraiser at my son's school. Within minutes, I had that hot little commodity in my fractured hand and found myself cozy in my chair on our deck overlooking the pristine landscape in front of me. I sat in quiet contemplation, relaxing simply by feeling the journal and pen in my lap.

As I asked myself what I would write about, I felt my pen scribbling across the back page of my empty journal. I wrote without hesitation or thought as I transferred words that seemed to be coming to me in the same manner. Halfway through the ninth page, the words came to a subtle end, and I saw my mother's name as though it was a letter. As I stared at her name in the middle of the page, my eyes scanned the previous pages, and I quickly recognized the printing to be practically identical to that of my mother who had passed away sixteen years earlier. Although it was I who had been doing the writing it seemed clear that the words had come from her from another realm and as they did, so did her style of penmanship. I felt goose bumps all over as I flipped back to the beginning and began to read what I had just written. As I had been writing, I had been unaware of what had been transpiring on the pages. As I read the letter that was addressed to me, I was amazed and astonished.

I didn't share this with anyone other than Steve and Dawson, for many months. I did, however, wake up every morning with a refreshed sense of purpose and a renewed sense of passion for writing. Writing became my painkiller and companion.

I awoke the next morning excited and enthusiastic to spend the day at home with my journal. I could not wait to write and see who came my way. I retraced my steps from the day before by sitting comfortably in my eagle's nest while listening to calming music. This time, I began the ritual of asking, in writing, for guidance and inviting anyone who was listening to share a message with me. To this day, I have always received a message from at least one of many guides, as long as I am sitting peacefully and simply ask. I always express my gratitude.

A Soulful Awakening

When I decide to channel in this manner, I begin by simply saying hello, offering gratitude, and asking a question. Words begin to fill the pages, and as they do, I am fully aware of my surroundings but completely engaged in the task at hand. I write without contemplation or hesitation until the message is complete and signed by the guide. I then close my journal and change my activity.

When and where I decide to read the latest message depends on the circumstance. If the message is directed to me, I usually read it within an hour. If the message is meant for someone else, I wait until I am able to read it to that individual. When this happens, I often feel waves of energy as I am sharing the message and break into a sweat. The messages are always positive and full of love; therefore, I am often unable to hold back tears as the energy engulfs me as I read.

Ustro introduced himself to me as one of my non-physical guides on day two. He mentioned that we knew each other here on earth, but he fell and died and was now here to assist me. He talked about the spiritual awakening that we are going through as a planet on a collective level. This was news to me at the time, but now, a year and a half later, that concept directs my life force.

Ustro became an integral part of my life until August 2013 when he moved on. Before he departed to aid another soul who was just beginning to awaken spiritually, he kindly introduced me to my new guide, Sal, but I was childish and didn't accept him until many months after Ustro left. I was shocked at how solemn I felt knowing that Ustro and I were parting ways.

The other guides, teachers, and protectors have come to me through various messages at various times. Some guides stand close to me, like ustro and sal, while others are more closely associated with other people who requested personal messages. Then a few, such as Ruby, Solomon, and Raphael, appear to be guardians on a much larger scope, encompassing many souls. It is my understanding that we are guided by many, each delivering their own insight in their own manner. For instance, Raphael introduced himself as a healer when called upon. He assists in the removal of toxicity from the human body by use of electromagnetic energy. We all have specific guides and teachers, yet there are no limitations to whom we may call upon. I have adopted the policy of accepting wisdom from whomever may deliver a response to my questions, as so far, all the information that has been shared has been beneficial and transformative. Again, I emphasize the importance of the message itself as opposed to where or from whom the message is coming.

When we allow ourselves to tune into the frequency of the non-physical realm and begin reestablishing relationships with our guides or the guides of others, our worlds expand tremendously. There is an astronomical amount of wisdom at our disposal at any given time; all we need is a little peace and quiet and an open heart and mind. You don't necessarily need to crash into a rock wall to hear your call from home. I took one for the team, so please spare yourself and enjoy this book as my gift to you.

There are many different voices contributing their messages throughout the book—each exhibiting their own unique spice and flare. For example, Sherman H. Harlow is eloquent and elegant as he delivers his teachings, while Ruby and Solomon are more straight and to the point. Ustro was gentle in his approach, as I was a newbie to the non-physical realm, while Sal is much more direct as he encourages my growth and the growth of others.

As time went on and I remained diligent in my practice of receiving the messages, they became more clear and fluid. Each guide has his or her own style of handwriting or printing. Some are smooth

A Soulful Awakening

and flowing, while others are more difficult to read. The first message I received from my grandfather Harold, I recognized his handwriting from when he was alive. Each guide has their own; they are individual while existing in unison wholly and completely. The following messages are the first two I received as my door to connection opened.

Linda (my mom):
I love you. You are okay. Live and let live. More to life and more to live for. I am always close by—we all are. You are on your way. I will help you and your family and all the others. I am here always like a fine film of dust sprinkled on your skin. I watch and wait for the time to be right, as it is now. You see, you are my angel as well.

Live with the truth in your heart, and you will always have what you need. You have it in front of you every day. Don't be discouraged, as it is easy to be at times. Let us guide you; trust in the universe, and you will be free. I am free and here—present. Your heart has been blocked, and now the key has been turned. Feel us, dear. We are here with you always. We guide you and try to help you along the way.

Trust in yourself, those you love, the sun and sky, and me. Ustro is here watching and listening and seeing. He will be here for a while but not forever. You knew him once before in a class. He died, and he now travels with you.

The door is now open. There is so much more to see, my love. You are so dear to me. It hurts you, I can see. But be strong, open your passageways, trust and be trusted, understand, be compassionate, try not to be sad or angry. Bring the happiness to others that you know you can and be proud of who you are and are becoming.

Stephanie Banks

You are so intricate and yet so simple. I feel so proud of you. You were my daughter, but I hand you over to the universe. You are a child of the universe, a student of order, a teacher of wisdom. You chose this course and are managing to stay on track. You are hurdling the obstacles where necessary.

Continually, look beyond your current depth of perception and you will see visions that only your true inner self is capable of creating. We create through visions of the unknown. We aspire to be enlightened by the forces that lie deep within ourselves. Reach in as deeply as you are able and pull out one puzzle piece at a time. There is a place for each piece, and each piece has a purpose, a meaning. Why does this piece fit here in this particular spot? How is it that this piece looks like it should fit but simply does not? If a puzzle piece is forced into a place where it simply is not meant to be, the entire puzzle is set incorrectly.

If we continue and pretend that the piece is, in fact, meant to be there eventually, we need to go back and remove the piece and start again. The further we go into the puzzle with an inadequate placement of pieces, the more difficult it will be to correct the problem. If we take the time and courage to place the pieces correctly from the onset, we will complete the puzzle much more efficiently and confidently.

Do not overlook the opportunity for growth. Seize the moment and open your gifts as they present themselves. Unwrap each gift with enthusiasm yet with care and concern. Discard the packaging and store your gifts in an efficient manner, as they will be plentiful. Think about all the gifts that you have been given but have lost.

Through true appreciation and gratitude, we learn to value each gift that comes our way. Life is a gift to others and ourselves. The sun is a gift to us daily, as is the earth on which we walk and the air of which we breathe. Each breath is a powerful gift of life on earth. Treasure your breath, and you will find new value in your existence here on earth. When darkness creeps into your soul, look for the light that will lead you back to gratitude. Emanate appreciation, and you will then notice it emanating all around you. Believe, my love, believe. I love you.

Ustro: *I fell. I am free. I live with you in your heart. I feel your pain and happiness, and it is my plan to aid your journey. You have had a tumultuous ride; things will become clear. Everyone we encounter has a teaching for us. We are here to learn even when it is difficult; in fact, that is when we take the largest strides. I did not want to die but did. My name is Ustro.*

You are in the heat of powerful times. There is a movement to bring clarity, reason, dimension, realism, and calmness to those who will be accepting. You are part of this movement. You have a strong and powerful soul, and feel there is more. Your grandfather is here—what a gentle soul he is. Quiet in the heart and mind and forever forgiving. You have lessons to learn from him, and most of them will be through your son.

You also need to heal, not just yourself but others. You know in your heart that you are a healer. Please do not deny that; it is a big part of who you are and a precious gift inherent to you. It mustn't be wasted. I have so much to say and am glad we are here; I enjoy your company and like your music. Clouds are important to you. Find the places and moments that bring you peace. Don't worry so much. I had that also.

Stef: Do I have other guides?

Ustro: *Yes. They stand a bit further from you than I do. They are your windbreaks. They are strong and comforting when you need them. They care for others; you share them, but they are always there to catch and guide you. You know there is more, you always have.*

Your mother is a wonderful soul. Very patient. She gets frustrated with you at times, because she believes that your eyes are closed too often. She tries to help you see her and us, but often you are distracted. It is difficult not to be distracted at times, I know, but you must make a stronger commitment with yourself to your consciousness.

I was assigned to you by you. You liked me in life, and we are of kindred spirits. I knew Katie. She comes to you from time to time, but there are others that require her presence. She is a funny one.

Don't resist. Just open yourself and listen to my words. Go with what is happening. You have lessons here to learn—you all do— from one another. Some will be clear and easy to see, so stay focused and in tune. The world is full of judgment, surprises, and hatred. Your mission amongst others is to teach the contrary. There is a lesson in everything. Everything. Everything we touch and smell and see. You are on the road you have chosen, so do not be afraid—be excited. You have so much time left and experiences yet to come.

These messages, these lessons are available to us all and provide insight into our life's experiences. At first, I simply wrote the messages as I heard them without much thought as to how they might relate to my life. Over time, I began to implement the lessons and to apply them not only to my current circumstances but also to my past experiences. I would sit quietly and recall certain times in my life that were challenging and difficult. I would consciously allow old, buried emotions to surface as I acknowledged those times in a different light.

As I applied the message I was receiving from the universe, from our guides and my higher self, I was able to cleanse that slate by removing any negative emotions that had become attached to that memory. I changed my perspective by gaining elevation in my vantage point. Simply by changing my lens from a zoom to a wide angle, I opened a door to a greater purpose and meaning in circumstance.

All experiences in life are learning lessons if we choose them to be so. We can wallow in self-pity by diving to the bottom of our emotional ocean, holding our breath, hoping to never surface to face our problems, but eventually we need to take a deep breath or we will drown in our sorrow. A more fulfilling option is to take hold of your life and remember that you have choices. You hold the key to understanding your chosen path and the lessons that come your way.

We are all connected and have stories that comprise our lives. Our characters and settings may differ from one another, but the themes are the same. Love, hate, jealousy, excitement, fear, pain, hope, sorrow, faith, and joy—we all share these emotions as we all develop relationships with others.

My hope is that you will find meaning and enlightenment in your own stories through reading mine. Find a way to relate these stories and messages to your experiences and apply the teachings from the non-physical realm in a way that brings you peace. As you learn to let go of what you have been holding on to, you will inevitably make room for growth. Through growth on a soul level, you will water and nourish the seeds you have sown for a more meaningful and successful life.

Chapter 3

Brushing Cheek-to-Cheek with Death

"Life is a magical expression of profound possibilities"
—Stephanie Banks

Not once, but twice, in one year I skirted life-threatening situations, both within four months of each other. Although at the time I viewed them both as inconvenient irritations intruding on my life, I now see clearly that they were wake-up calls. I have always been one to jump out of a deep slumber rather than wake up gradually, and my spiritual awakening has proven to be no different.

Four months prior to my bike accident, I received an unexpected birthday gift in April 2012. This gift turned my life and the vision that I had for my life upside down for many months.

A Soulful Awakening

Many parts of Canada, including Kamloops, are prime habitats for the dreaded wood tick. As a landscaper and country dweller, it is not unheard of to find this deadly tiny critter attached to my body from time to time. In the spring of 2012, I removed three. The second one I discovered while I was getting dressed for my fortieth birthday celebration.

I discovered the speck of a creature deeply embedded in my skin just above my rib cage in line with the bottom strap of my sports bra. Without a second thought, I pinched its body and ripped it out. Unfortunately, its head separated from its body, leaving the body between my fingers with the head still under my skin. With nail scissors and tweezers, I began cutting away the skin until I was able to remove the head. I tossed both parts of the tick in the toilet and flushed them away, believing that that was the end of it.

A week or so later, I was at a jobsite and asked to use the homeowner's washroom. As I was washing my hands, I noticed another tick on my shoulder. This one was not as embedded and was easier to remove. I took this time to lift my shirt and bra and take a look at the bite mark from the one I had found on my birthday.

I felt instant anxiety as I saw a bright red ring encircling the bite mark, similar to that of a ringworm. I didn't know anything about Lyme disease at the time, but as quickly as I discovered the mark, I knew conclusively in my heart that this was my new challenge to overcome.

That evening, I spent hours on the Internet researching Lyme disease, and from what I could tell, the only true way to determine if a person had been infected was if a red itchy ring appeared. Most people who are infected go undiagnosed for years, as only six percent of those of us who are infected actually develop the red ring. That red ring was, in fact, my birthday gift, because without its appearance, I would have become a long-term victim along with countless others, who have no idea where their symptoms originated from. Consequently, their lives become unmanageable.

One of the symptoms of Lyme is unbearable fatigue combined with excruciating headaches. These inevitably become debilitating, and curing them in the later stages becomes extremely difficult.

The victim is often unable to function normally in all aspects of life, and most become dependant on others for full support physically, emotionally, and financially. By the time the physical symptoms present themselves, so much time has elapsed since the tick was removed that most do not correlate the two, making the diagnosis complicated, if at all possible. In my case, I was fortunate to see the red mark develop as well as the symptoms appearing within the first two weeks.

On the first evening upon discovery, I sent a picture of the bite and marking to a client whose husband is a doctor. He happened to be working in the emergency room that evening, and although he didn't seem concerned initially, his tune changed once he had seen the picture. Upon his advice, I drove into the hospital and met with him. We discussed Lyme disease, the medical testing for it, and the rate of occurrence of the disease in British Columbia, which is only one out of one hundred thousand. I believe that number is inaccurate, as most cases go undiagnosed.

The doctor set me up with a heavy twenty-one-day dose of antibiotics, which would hopefully cure me. I have mixed feelings about conventional medicine, and antibiotics are not something I choose to take without great contemplation. I spent the next forty-eight hours researching antibiotics and the effects of them with Lyme disease. The information I was finding was not building my confidence, as most victims found them ineffective and repeated doses multiple times per year for years without significant results.

During this time, I had been guided to an alternative treatment, which I began to research as well. I spent an afternoon with a gentleman who had been trained with this formula and was an advocate for the product. He had one case study, which was more than I had seen for antibiotics, where he had successfully treated a patient who suffered from later stages of Lyme. He was anti-antibiotics, but at the end of our discussions, he encouraged me to do what I felt would help me the most. I left his organic farm with a renewed sense of hope and a bag of herbs and tinctures.

The beginning stages of the disease were presenting themselves in the form of fatigue and headaches. I was unable to get through a day without crashing on my friends' or family's couches for a few hours and popping Advil. I felt afraid, cheated, and angry. I was only forty years old and was facing the prospects of a long-term illness that didn't seem to be curable. I knew I needed to make a decision quickly regarding what form of treatment I would choose to take.

As I filtered through all the information I had gathered, I decided in the end to use both the antibiotics and the alternative treatment. Both of which were twenty-one-day protocols. I began on day one with an incredible sense of determination. I was determined to stop this awful disease in its tracks by eliminating all remnants of it completely from my body.

My thought was that the harshness and abruptness of the antibiotics would have the initial impact and power required to slow the process enough that the Lyme would be kept in the stage-one compartment of this multi-staged disease. I did not have enough faith that the antibiotics would seal the deal in the end; hence, my choice to incorporate the alternative treatment, which, in my opinion, would carry the treatment through to the bitter end, resulting in a complete cure.

The treatment themselves became a full-time job, as the antibiotics required that I ate food at the same time each day while the alternative was to be taken in the form of a liquid ounce every hour on the hour for twelve hours per day for twenty-one days. I continued to work full time operating my business alongside my brother, as well as trying my best to contribute to my role as a parent and spouse.

The alarm clock on my phone was set to remind me throughout the day of my obligation to dose myself with some form of treatment. The alternative concoction holds the record to this day as the most disgusting taste I have ever had to swallow. Every hour when I was to take my ounce, I would cringe and dry heave at the thought. It took every ounce of determination to down every ounce of that drink. The taste is indescribable. It resembles nothing of comparison; therefore, unless you were to drink it yourself, you will never truly know the taste.

Halfway through my twenty-one days of anguish, I became so fed up and irritated that I literally threw my water bottle—which held this horrific concoction—as far as I could throw it. I took the rest of that day off of the treatment and allowed myself a short hiatus. This short but impactful vacation was just enough to reignite my spark to get well. I awoke the following morning refreshed and realigned with my purpose for all these medicines and my ultimate goal. I knew in my heart and mind that I was going to win this battle. I was determined, and as miserable as I was at times I never doubted my ability to heal myself.

A Soulful Awakening

I attribute this powerful belief to a Deepak Chopra meditation that I repeated many times throughout that month. I have always loved the word *homeostasis* but never knew exactly what it meant until that meditation. I could write an entire chapter on the value of meditation, but I think that will have to wait until next time. Suffice it to say, there is an abundance of knowledge, wisdom, and healing available to us all, which becomes more available to us with a quiet mind. The higher self responds remarkably well to peace and quiet. It is in these moments when we are best able to soak in the healing rays of the universe and exchange our negatively charged cells with newly revitalized energy to fill our bodies and spirits.

I'm not exactly sure when Lyme and I parted ways, but it was an intense, short-lived relationship that was simply not meant to be. I spoke loudly and clearly both verbally and in my mind to Lyme and told it why I did not want it in my life. Like a persistent ex-boyfriend, it tried everything it could think of to remain together, but eventually I made myself clear. To this day, I don't have any remnants of this disease. Candida, however, has become my most challenging lesson to date. One thing is certain to me now: antibiotics do, in fact, wreak havoc on the body. At least, they did to mine. Twenty-one days of antibiotics and two years of nearly constant signs of yeast overgrowth.

I will never know conclusively whether or not I required the antibiotics, but I have always been one to cover all my bases. At the time of medicating, I did believe wholeheartedly in my choice of remedies, and that, to me, is a necessary ingredient required in order to truly heal oneself. This process of self-healing is referred to as Homeostasis by the medical community and was first introduced to me through that Deepak Chopra meditation that I faithfully did every morning during that recovery period. Thank you, Deepak.

Four months after my encounter with Lyme disease, I brushed death again with my bike. Although at the time I did not realize how close I had come when hitting that rock face, I have since been shown very clearly what I experienced in that moment of impact.

Shortly after my accident while I was exploring my new gift of channeling, Steve and I decided to try to channel verbally. We sat with our close friend, Cameron, who has spent the majority of his life growing both himself and others spiritually. We spent five hours with him one evening, and I began by reading him some of the messages I had received in hopes of acquainting Cameron with some of the guides who had come through. He then led me into a deep meditative state in a way that I was able to experience and recall certain aspects that had transpired. I didn't know what to expect, so I entered into the process by releasing any and all expectations.

Ruby was the first guide to come through that evening. As he began to use my voice to relay his messages, I recall feeling as though my physical body was weightless in the chair. I saw an image of myself sitting in a small fishing boat in a bay beneath an enormous cliff. It was a beautiful place to be, and it was from here that I witnessed the channeling of Ruby and Solomon.

Cameron prompted them with questions we had decided to ask and Ruby and Solomon responded with incredible wisdom and knowing. As they were responding, I could hear my voice, yet it was clearly not me manifesting the words.

At one point, I felt my body begin to spin. I felt as though I was in a vortex being pulled to one side. I could feel my hand gripping the arm of the chair. It felt as though my hand was cramped and my knuckles were stiff. As I sat spinning in my own world, Ruby spoke of my bike crash. He told us that I had died momentarily but chose to come back; in that moment, I was made privy to my life's plan and purpose. I do not have a distinct recollection of seeing that plan but I do know that I returned from that trip to Whistler a much different person. My purpose for life has become one of a more natural role, a concerned and caring inhabitant of this world and universe. I am now an awakened soul and hope I can help stir that in you.

Unfortunately, we did not record this session, as we were unprepared for what was to transpire. It was not until after the session when I was completely present that Steve and Cameron relayed to me what they had heard. We discussed my death and how amazed they were that I had been with Ruby and my other guides and had chosen to return. As I digested this information during the months to come I experienced a profound transition in how I defined life and my purpose within this physical existence. I developed a new appreciation for life and all that it encompasses both physically and non-physically. I also felt an urge to hear about this life and death experience from Ruby in such a way that I would best be able to have reference to his words at any given time, therefore I asked one day in my morning writing. The following is a reiteration from Ruby of what transpired on that day.

Ruby: *Stephie, your life was shown to you from start to finish. This is often what happens as your soul reunites with the source of all existence. Oftentimes, one experiences all aspects of their soul as physicality is disrupted and recalculated. There is a calculation and quantification process in everything. Death of the physical body is no different. It is a tremendously powerful experience, as is birth. Therefore, profound transformations are not rare. Unique, yes, but not rare.*

Some remember the experience, and this memory lives lifetimes, because, remember, remembering does not actually exist—if it did, our truth of time and space would be different. Everything is happening in the present, so remembering is not real in totality. It is, however, very real in the experience of living as a human on earth; therefore, I will speak in your language.

Your remembrance of this event comes in the form of transformation of your thoughts and actions. You have chosen to remember through inner dialogue with your higher self, as well as those that guide you as you ask them to. Your impact was sudden and harsh. The physical body is not designed to survive such velocity combined with impact; however, the higher self does not die and has created your vessel. Your higher self makes the final decision as to whether or not the physical body will die and the soul will return to source to begin creation yet again.

As this process is being calculated and quantified, the soul is guided by many souls through the process. There are endless aspects of one's soul in combination with all souls, and each of these aspects is unique to that individual soul. How these individual souls interact and exchange with all souls is different than that of others. Souls are malleable, forever changing. Remember: remembering and forever do not exist in totality. All souls experience some sort of profound change through trauma of any kind.

The meaning of trauma is to be injured emotionally and physically, simultaneously. When trauma is present, the soul kicks into high gear and aids in the release of pressure buildup in the form of energy. The quickest and most effective way to release traumatic pressure is through a direct line to source. Source absorbs this pressure and transforms it back to pure form—pure energy—while releasing it back to the universe. As the traumatized soul experiences this pressure release, it is also reenergized with the purified energy. This process happens instantaneously; however, it takes time, as you know it, for the human vessel to catch up and experience fully the transformation. There are times when the soul chooses not to remember any of the events at all. This is simply part of that soul's master plan. Others choose to remember vividly every detail of their experience. The ways in which humans choose to transform from these traumatic moments are countless.

Yours, my dear, is true to you. This is your story, your love affair with life. Share it as you choose.

Stef: Thank you, Ruby. It is all so interesting and amazing. During our live channeling session, you reminded me of specific details of what happened during the impact that day. Could you please reiterate that to me today? Forgive me. I cannot remember what you told me.

Ruby: *Dear child, you were engaged with source through a direct channel, and from this vantage point you saw your eternal life as well as your human life. You did not hesitate to reinstate with your physical body. You interpreted your accident as you had formerly designed yourself to, as a reconnection to all that is through trauma. Trauma is a tool designed by the collective consciousness of life on earth. This tool, trauma, is used when the soul urns and aches to reconnect with source energy. In your particular experience, you requested a wake-up call at this stage in your life if you had not awoken yet.*

This is a common and frequent method used by humans. You and I glided through yourself and all existence as your physical body embedded itself in the gully momentarily.

Although the time frame seems short in linear time, this experience we shared was endless. You asked to see the others who guide you daily, and together we witnessed your soul reignite and reunite with all. You chose to experience life through your direct line and made a conscious decision to assist others in the same way. This was your driving force that catapulted you back to earthly reality. You chose not to see or experience too much, as you did not want to reconsider your choice.

Your heart stopped briefly as trauma built up and created blockages, but as quickly as it stopped, it resumed again as your soul made the final decision to resume life on earth—but with a renewed sense of self. You chose to hold conscious thought and intent in your heart in such a way that it would drive your existence.

Chapter 4

The Magic of Synchronicities

"Life isn't as serious as the mind makes it out to be."
—Eckhart Tolle

My life, this time around, began on April 18, 1972, in the Calgary Children's Hospital. My mom came from a middle- to upper-class home in the outskirts of Toronto. Born in 1943, she would remain an only child until 1996 when her body succumbed to lymphoma.

Her parents, my grandparents, Eileen and Harold, migrated from England to Canada with a sea captain's trunk and the desire and resilience to create a new life for themselves in Canada. My grandfather was a chartered accountant who began his climb up the corporate ladder of Ontario Hydro. I remember my brother implying that Grandpa didn't thoroughly enjoy his profession, as the corporate world was severely deficient in the values that my grandfather lived by. The disconnection that resided within my grandfather created disharmony within his mind and soul. I wonder how many people feel this way?

My grandfather was an integral part of my life until I was fourteen years old. He was kind, gentle, knowledgeable, and encouraging and interested in all aspects of our lives. Ustro described him to me as "a powerful soul who is quiet in the heart and mind and forever forgiving." What a wonderful way to be looked upon.

I was named after my grandmother, Eileen White. She passed away when I was in grade seven; this was the second time in her life that her heart stopped ticking. She was born with many health issues, one of which was severe debilitating asthma. When she and my grandfather decided to have children, their doctors warned them that childbirth could quite possibly bring death upon both her and the newborn. The force within Eileen to bring a child into the world was too strong to ignore, and together my grandparents created my mother Linda.

As the doctors had predicted, there were major complications during the delivery and my grandmother died. Her heart stopped beating as she delivered another soul into our world. As the doctors worked diligently to revive Eileen, her heart picked up where it had left off and life within her physical body resumed. My grandparents loved and cherished each other, and gave complete gratitude for each day that they lived thereafter.

My mother Linda was raised in a home with a solid foundation based on love, respect, and trust. The same foundation has been passed onto our home, and we will pass this onto our son in hopes of keeping the tradition alive.

My mom led a very interesting and exciting life as a graceful woman, who was an inspiration to many women of her time. She was a leader and a true believer in equality for all souls. She was intuitive and tried as best as she could to allow her inner self to guide her through her life's journey. She encouraged both my brother and me to do the same as she often pressed her index finger firmly into our navels while saying, "Trust in your gut, and go with your instinct. Follow and trust your intuition, and you will always be led in the correct direction."

She met my biological father Steve while attending high school in Toronto. They became high school sweethearts and would later marry and have a family. They were both ambitious and parted ways briefly to pursue their post-secondary educations. My mom moved to New York City and attended the School of Fine Arts.

As a little girl, I was enthralled by her stories of living in such a vibrant and active city. As a fan of *The Cosby Show*, I especially enjoyed her stories about her friendship with Bill Cosby. She had an amazing sense of humor, and I will always remember the times that she would make herself laugh so hard that she would drop to the ground, roll around, and clutch her stomach. These were happy memories, and I truly wish that I would witness more people in this position of pure joy.

My father pursued an education in law, and once they had both completed their degrees, they married and moved to Calgary, Alberta, to begin a new chapter in their lives. My father practiced law while our mother became a mom. My brother was the first to arrive in June of 1970, and I came along shortly after.

My father was an up-and-coming lawyer, we had two dogs, a modest home in the city, and everything but the white picket fence. Life changed drastically for us all just prior to my second birthday when my father was diagnosed with multiple sclerosis. The fear that developed within my father was too great for him, and as a result, he chose to travel the rest of his life on a solo journey without the love and support that his family could have offered. My mother was heartbroken as her marriage came to a screeching halt with very little closure, if any at all.

A few years later, our mother met Rudi while partaking on a hiking trip, and they soon married. They remained married for seventeen years, and Rudi adopted us as his own. He was a loving and caring father and is very present in our lives today. I didn't have contact with my biological father until I was twenty-four—two months before my mother passed away.

After my father's diagnosis of MS, he moved to Guadalajara, New Mexico, as the weather is more conducive to the disease he was suffering from. He was unable to work, became dependent on others for basic needs, and turned to Christianity as an avenue to find solace in his life. His life there came to a close approximately twenty years later, shortly before my mother's death.

Steve was devoted to attending his local church two days a week while in New Mexico, and after being absent for months, the pastor of his church decided to look for him. Sadly, he discovered my father close to death, lying in his bed in his trailer. His body was covered in bedsores, his teeth had become rotten—some of which had fallen out—and his body was severely emaciated. The bed in which he lay was drenched in his own excrement.

On the couch in the living room, the pastor found a woman passed out with a bottle in her hand and an overflowing ashtray by her cheek. She had spent his disability money on alcohol and cigarettes while his body starved for nourishment and care.

It is difficult to comprehend the lack of compassion and care that existed within that trailer, but this is the harsh reality that exists within our world. The pastor contacted Steve's next of kin, and he was immediately flown to Hamilton, Ontario, with only his shirt

A Soulful Awakening

on his back and a life of despair to come to terms with. After a substantial lengthy recovery and over $10,000 in dental surgery, my father was placed in an aided care facility, which is where he still resides today.

During the spring of 1996, my mother was taken into surgery to remove a lump from the base of her spine. This surgery led to her demise, and her physical body succumbed to cancer on November 2, 1996, with my brother, her dog Tai-Li, and me by her side. I was a mere twenty-four years young.

Prior to her death, before the surgery, she was placed on a waiting list for one of two hospitals located in different cities. One was in London, Ontario, and the other in Hamilton, Ontario. She was hoping to be placed in London, as this city is closer in proximity to our hometown of Stratford. To her disappointment, Hamilton became her home for many months. At this point, my life took a dramatic turn.

At the time, I was living in Victoria, British Columbia, enjoying a carefree life as a young adult. I was twenty-four and spent the majority of my time hiking along the West Coast and hanging out on the beach. My move back to Ontario happened quickly, and the decision to go home was made without much contemplation. I knew where I needed to be and why. This new chapter in my life was created by fate, and I was on a journey that I believe was created long before.

I took over my mom's life as best as I could with the loving support of my boyfriend at the time, who chose to move to Ontario with me. He was and still is a beautiful, caring soul. Together we managed my mother's home, adopted her dog as our own, and traveled over four hours a day—sometimes twice a day—to visit my mom in Hamilton. We were fortunate to have the emotional support of many of my mom's friends and co-workers. They were all truly a blessing.

By this time, my father Steve had already been moved to Hamilton as well and was settling into his new surroundings. The view from my mother's hospital room encompassed the building where her high school sweetheart, the father of her children, now resided. She gazed over the valley toward this building for many months before it came to our attention that this was Steve's new home.

I distinctly remember the feeling of complete bewilderment at how the universe operates when I heard this news. How could this have come to be that both my parents were placed in care facilities just five minutes from one another in a city that neither had a connection to twenty-two years after their last correspondence? I pondered this question many times for many years. I now realize quite clearly that there are no coincidences. Irony is not congruent with spiritualism; the universe is structured and methodical.

There was a reason why Linda and Steve were reunited in this way. Although they didn't see each other in person, they did spend time on the phone and managed to close a chapter that had been left unfinished for far too long. As much as I believe in the order and structure that exists within the universe, I also strongly believe that there is a message in everything and everyone we experience. If our lesson has not been learned when the time to leave this earth comes, then we will have to come back and learn that lesson at some point. This is okay. This is simply how I believe the universe functions. Learning is continual and cyclical; there are no exemptions to learning.

As we learn the universal lessons of love, compassion, patience, gratitude, acceptance, creativity, joy, and many more, our lives become richer and more meaningful. When we take the time to challenge ourselves to live these lessons, as we learn about them, we create harmony amongst our mind, body, and soul. For true happiness to exist within our hearts, we need this unity to exist.

After many months of treatment, we began to accept that our mother was not going to pull through. She asked to be moved home from the hospital and be close to her loved ones and her dog. She had a few decent weeks filled with many meaningful moments until her body began to shut down.

The day that she passed, our mom opened her eyes for the first time in over a week as she asked for my brother and I to be by her side. Her dog was already lying loyally under her bed. Although her physical body had been in a coma for over a week, she was completely coherent and seemed comfortable. As we held her hand, she spoke softly of the other side and of the lady who was there to hold her hand as she transitioned. She drifted between our world and another for a few minutes before she took a leap of faith in unison with her last breath on earth and uttered the words, "It's all crap!" Hmmm. Your guess is as good as mine.

On that cold autumn day in November of 1996, my mom made her transition. Although she was at peace, she was reluctant to let go. I assured her that she was going to a beautiful, loving place. At the time, I didn't know this to be true, but I was hopeful that this world of which I spoke existed.

Stef: Good afternoon, guides, teachers, and protectors. As I wrote the story about my mom and Steve, I was amazed by the coincidence of them both residing in the same city at the same time because of their individual paths relating to their health. I know that they had unfinished business, so to speak, which is why I believe they were brought together in this way. Some synchronicities in life seem more apparent and imperative than others. Does anyone have a message to share on coincidences, synchronicities, or miracles?

Sal: *The world is there for everyone to explore and create magic if you so choose. The universe is forever providing clues into our collective and individual consciousness. These clues provide guidance, and if recognized and used as they appear, they create flow and balance. They link actions and transactions in a way that only synchronicities are able.*

They are always present and present themselves as just that. Presents, gifts for you to enjoy and use at your ultimate disposal. By ignoring these gifts, you may limit your life and your expansion in some way. You will still be capable of reaching your goals and aspirations; however, the synchronistic events that are offered are a simple form of acceleration. Think of them as a cheat sheet for a test or a short form in a math equation.

Some people are accustomed to learning and reaching their goals by taking the long road around obstacles and through life, while others are more apt to look for the shortcuts. As you begin to take notice of these coincidences, these seemingly odd occurrences that appear precisely at the right moment in your time, you will begin to notice more.

An example would go like this: imagine yourself at the supermarket. As you fill your cart with all your desired goods, the ones at the bottom become buried and inaccessible unless you unload your cart. As you unload this cart of gifts in the form of food, you unveil the gifts at the bottom. Synchronicities work in a similar manner. As you dismiss coincidences as merely fun and worthy of a good story but nothing more, they remain in your spiritual shopping cart but become buried and oftentimes forgotten about.

Do not judge a book by the cover. A coincidence may seem small and insignificant at the time it appears, but just like any puzzle, all the pieces put together create a whole—no matter how big, small, colorful, or plain they may be. If you toss a small, plain puzzle piece in the garbage because it appears insignificant to you at the time, you will find later as your puzzle nears completion that the little piece is very important to the puzzle as a whole.

One synchronicity always leads to another and to another and to another. There are an infinite number of these gifts available to all; many have been created by the individual receiving them, prior to incarnation. They are reminders set in place to help you stay on track and to aid you on your journey of following your excitements.

Have fun with this aspect of life and allow their magic to aid in your creation of your life, both on earth and in a universal sense.

Stef: Good evening, universe. Does anyone have a message to share on transitioning from life to death, as we understand it here on earth?

Hazel: *I am free. I am love. I am compassion and warmth when the wind blows the opposite. I died with peace in my heart and calm surrounding my soul. I was surrounded by the love and understanding of my family. When we allow love from all levels to enter our hearts, we accept forgiveness of our wrong doings and accept ourselves as the human beings that we are. We are not perfect, we are not pure, we are not authentic at all times, because we are here on earth to learn as much about ourselves and our universe as we possibly can.*

I made the transition from the realm of earth to nirvana with ease, as my conscious was clear. I forgave myself for my mistakes as they arose throughout my life. I did not leave any doors closed if there was dust left in the room that needed to settle and later cleared. My family was nonjudgmental of my choices; they loved me unconditionally, as I did them. We walked through our lives in unison and harmony. I was in need of nothing, because in this lifetime I lived a privileged and pain-free lifestyle.

If we wake each day and greet it with good intentions, we will pass on through this same ray of sunshine. If we live in the shadows of darkness, we will still have to find our own ray of light before we find complete transition. Learn to forgive yourself and others, as this is a crucial lesson. This lesson affects so many aspects of ourselves. It affects how we integrate our lives with others, it affects how we communicate, and it affects how we operate on a daily basis. If we are holding a grudge, it will feel like an anchor on our soul. If we feel resentment in any way, it will feel like we are bathing in toxic waste.

There is no use for resentment or revenge; learn to let things go daily, as each day brings forth an opportunity for growth and renewed awareness. If we deal with our "stuff" daily, we will have the freedom to move effortlessly to the next phase of our continual existence when our day of transition comes. It is always important to surround yourself with friends and family who share the same ideas, as this will contribute to both ascension and transition. Regardless of how easy or difficult a transition may be, remember both are happening through the loving hands of understanding and compassion. It is simply an easier task if we understand these aspects of the soul while alive in our physical bodies. Do not fear being alive. Do not fear death. Do not allow fear to engage in your thoughts or dictate an emotional storm, as the wreckage will be costly and draining to the ecology of the soul.

Chapter 5

Life at Grenville

"The only limits you have are the limits you believe."
—Wayne Dyer

Katie and I met during our first year of high school. We shared a class, and the first time that I heard her laugh and witnessed her smile, I thought she was the coolest girl I had ever set eyes upon. She was beautiful in a tomboy-ish way, and her eyes sparkled as though the universe had planted diamonds in them at birth. Her hair shimmered as it hung across her cheeks and kissed her shoulders. We had yet to meet until that day in class when she turned while slouched at her desk and smiled directly at me as though we were old-time friends. Our friendship was as instantaneous as that first glance. We became inseparable allies as we marched through our days of high school.

Her family became my second family, and mine became hers. Both our parents were advocates of private schooling, and as grade nine neared its commencement, discussions began about the two of us going to boarding school together. The decision was made by all of us, and grade ten marked the beginning of our private school experience at a Christian college.

The memories that I have from this school are as mixed as any breed of dog adopted from the pound. The life we lived at this school prepared me for so much more than I could ever put into words. My family was not of a religious background; however, I was raised to believe in the individual right to create my own story, my own belief system, and my own form of prayer. I was encouraged to believe in the universe in its entirety and to respect the beliefs of others no matter how they may differ from my own. This school we found ourselves attending did not share the same value system. The rules were strict, and the consequences for breaking them were worse.

We were not bad kids; we were simply teenagers who were being stifled from expressing ourselves. The school was Christian-based, and I believe that their primary objective was to convert all those in attendance to the ways of the hierarchy to whom we bowed within the walls of that magnificent, old stone building. The ways that the school operated seemed outdated and confined to a belief system that forbids kids such as Katie and myself from developing our own thoughts, our own stories, and our own individual notions of the meaning of God.

It soon became clear that if we didn't choose to conform to a path where we walked hand-in-hand with a God that we were told to believe in, our lives at our Christian college would become miserable. As much as we both tried to act as we were told, speak the way we were expected, and bow to those who insisted upon it, we still didn't meet the expectations of our deans and headmaster.

Katie and I were separated within the first few months of grade ten by those who ruled our lives. We were told that we were bad influences on one another, and therefore, our friends at the school would be chosen for us. If we were caught talking to each other or others we were told to stay away from, we would be disciplined

A Soulful Awakening

accordingly. The diamonds I had seen in Katie's eyes had been stolen by those who were meant to be inspiring, educating, and nurturing. One day blurred into the next as we struggled to simply survive each day without torment from the nuns, teachers, deans, coaches, and the dreaded headmasters and his wife, who seemed to live in her full-length fur coat. I suppose there was plenty of leftover pennies from our hefty tuitions.

Katie and I were both athletes, so we decided in secrecy to join as many teams as possible. This would allow us the opportunity to share time and space during practices, games, and competitions. We lived at the school, so joining these activities granted us "get of jail free" cards whenever we had games to play or meets to compete in.

As we traveled playing basketball, track and field, and skate skiing, it became apparent by talking to those we encountered that our school had created a stigma for itself that would later prove to be true. Although we were strictly prohibited from socializing with our opponents, there were brief moments of freedom in the change rooms when the other girls would bombard us with questions regarding life behind our school gates. The stories that had circulated within the surrounding communities gave our school a reputation of cruelty, emotional abuse, and a cult-like nature. These stories I knew to be true on many levels, yet at the same time, I willingly chose to return the following year.

During my first year, I was put on the legendary "discipline" numerous times. It took very little to be assigned to "discipline". Just as the word implies, it was used as a disciplinary tool used to attempt to transform the bad apples into good, obedient Christians. Discipline did not discriminate. Christian kids were also put on discipline from time to time for various reasons. The most common reason was for fraternizing with the outside kids. The outside kids constituted the majority of the school's population. We were the kids that didn't grow up at the school or at the affiliated community.

This community, as I understood it, was a small-gated community of people who generally do not mix with the outside world. The children who were born and raised in this community were sheltered from the outside world completely. They were forced to adopt the religious beliefs and behaviors of their elders without question. I befriended a few of these kids, and we quietly exchanged stories about our lives, our families, our fears, and our ambitions. Many were too fearful to run away, even though this was what they longed to do.

There were times when we would be caught talking and these children would be sentenced to discipline for extended periods of time. I always felt a pang of guilt during these times for playing my part in these forbidden conversations. I remember distinctly a new girl from the affiliated community who was assigned to my room for a short period. After the lights were turned off at nighttime, I offered her support as she suffered through weeks of withdrawal from prescription painkillers. She shared stories with me about her upbringing that would have shattered anybody's soul. Hers was most definitely broken and in need of repair. I often wonder about her and where she is today.

A typical day at school began in the wee hours of the morning, well before the earliest birds had risen. We were allotted seven-minute showers, which we signed up for the night before. Once we were showered and dressed in our uniforms, we were checked over by the floor dean, who made sure that we were wearing a slip beneath our kilts and that our kilts hung below our knees. We would then head to the dining hall for breakfast and sit at our assigned tables and wait for the headmaster and his wife to enter.

At this point, we would all bow and remain standing until they were both comfortably seated at their elevated table.

Breakfast was followed by morning prayers and setting the tables for our next meal. We would then spend the day in class. After class, we were given free time, which for me was always occupied with sports practices. Dinner was next, and then an hour of free time, followed by two hours of mandatory study hall. The evening ended with a brief prayer session in the chapel that was referred to as complin. I have fond memories of this quiet time, because Katie and I would often exchange a smile and I would take a few moments to give my own gratitude in my own manner without interruptions. After complin, we would return to our dorms and get ready for bed. The floor dean would turn our lights off one by one and the most uncomplicated tranquil period of our day would begin: sleep.

A day on discipline looked much different than this. Our days began even earlier, and instead of having a shower, we went straight to chores. We did not wear a uniform, but rather plain clothes. The idea being that we would stand out from the rest and everyone was made aware of who was on discipline. Staff members strictly prohibited communicating in any way with someone in plain clothes. We would not eat meals in the dining hall, nor would we attend classes. Bowing was still mandatory, and that we did a lot of. We would eat and study in the staff quarters while under constant supervision. Sports practices were missed and replaced with more chores. These days were long, dark, and emotionally draining. We were drilled by various staff members and the headmaster about our actions, or lack thereof, and how those actions would lead us to the depths of hell if we continued to be disobedient.

These times were a test of my inner strength and will. I would consciously spend time training myself to not allow these people to break my spirit, as I had witnessed this happening to many around me. I was open with my parents about all aspects of the school, good and bad, and their support was a wonderful example of their unconditional love for me. I was not obligated to stay, but I was aware of the financial investment that my grandparents had made for my education, so I decided to test myself further by choosing to finish the year.

Near the end of our first year, the formation of a special bike team was announced. This team would consist of nine boys and nine girls who would represent our school. The team would be sponsored by numerous big businesses, and the goal would be to raise money for Big Brothers Big Sisters of Canada. The team members would train for a year, preparing to bike from the East Coast to the West Coast of the country. As soon as Katie and I heard about the team, we both knew that we needed to be a part of such a fantastic opportunity. As two athletic girls, we didn't have any problems being chosen for the team; however, committing to this bike team came with a price tag: we would also have to commit to another year at our school. We discussed our options and unanimously decided that it was worth it.

Our second year began, and intense training continued as our worlds revolved around this biking adventure. Our bikes and gear were sponsored along with a logbook that we used to document all of our training time. We were expected to train over the summer months as well, which I did for a minimum of two to three hours every day. About half of the members were staff kids and the other half were outside kids. In hindsight, I now believe that the outside kids wouldn't have been given such an opportunity had there been enough athletically inclined staff kids to comprise the team in the first place.

A Soulful Awakening

We all poured our hearts and souls into the team's objectives, and once school began the following year, we were in amazing shape. The training intensified as word got out about the bike trip and sponsors began to pour in. We traveled to Quebec to climb our bikes up the grueling hills of Gatineau Park and many other uniquely challenging areas. We gave everything we had to this team for almost a full year before things began to crumble.

The pressure to become worshippers of God in the way that our superiors expected us to be became unbearable. We had become masters of living double lives in order to survive. We were angels in my eyes. We were focused on our education and athletic endeavors, we were cordial to everyone, and our kilts always hung below our knees. We were respectful to our elders, we bowed on command, and we inspired the younger ones in many ways. I continued to pray in their way as well as my own. This was not enough.

Chapter 6

The Beginning of the End

*"Be impeccable with your word, speak with integrity,
say only what you mean,
avoid using the word to speak against yourself
or gossip about others.
Use the power of your word in the direction of truth and love."*
—Miguel Angel Ruiz

A mandatory meeting was called for all team members. It was to be held in the living quarters of our headmaster and his wife. This was not a space that we commoners frequented; therefore, we anticipated a serious meeting. As we all gathered at the knees of our hierarchy and his wife, his smile looked as crooked as his intentions. He announced that there were certain team members who would not continue on this journey unless we could prove our love for Jesus Christ.

We were singled out one by one and asked to stand before the group and bellow as loud as we could, "I love Jesus!" For some, including a close friend Christina, this was too much to bear, and with tears streaming down her cheeks, she was asked to accept her dismissal from the team, which she had trained with for so long. I watched my friend crumble before me as her spirit was crushed and scarred by such unloving souls as these that held our fates in their slimy, self-indulgent fists. My turn inevitably came. I stood with both feet firmly planted as I grounded myself through the souls of my feet to the core of the earth. I closed my eyes and bellowed the words I was told to: "I love Jesus!" My place on the team was secure for the time being. Katie did the same, and together we walked in silent disbelief back to our dorms.

The next few days were tarnished by an unnerving silence among the team. Those who didn't return were replaced with inadequately trained Christian kids. Although they were not fit for such a team physically, they were there because of their faith.

At the same time as all of this nonsense, Katie, Christina, and I were also involved heavily in cross-country skate skiing. We practiced daily after school and for many hours on the weekends. I have wonderful fond memories of the three of us sneaking off to practice in tranquility as we skied through the woods that bordered our school. At times, we would stop to climb our favorite tree and sit quietly with one another while pondering our own individual circumstances. We never spoke of the time at the headmaster's quarters. Christina did not judge us, and we did not judge her. We were simply living our own young lives to the best of our capabilities. These days were infrequent but beautiful moments in time.

Our diligence and hard work paid off in this sport, as the three of us qualified for the Ontario provincial skate-skiing meet. A fourth person also qualified, so we formed a four-person relay team to compete at this high-level event. No matter how hard the school tried, we managed to become inseparable in our own way. Our training continued alongside and in conjunction with the cross-country bike team. We were in the best shape of our lives, and I felt like I had managed to maintain the image that was mandatory, at least to that point.

There were only weeks left before the provincials and just over two months remaining before we would launch into a once-in-a-lifetime opportunity to experience our awesome country as we peddled our way across it. My anticipation for both was growing as I spent my days training, studying, eating, and sleeping. These grueling days energized my soul and brought meaning to the seemingly illogical nonsense that transpired around me daily.

All of my dreams came crashing down around me shortly after a three-day weekend that we spent with our friend in the sleepy town of Smith Falls. Katie and I spent most of our breaks from the school here because our hometown was too far away. We had decided to go to a party on the Saturday night before, and one of us stumbled across a telephone calling card on our way home. The card had fifteen dollars worth of time, so we decided to split it three ways when we returned to school. At school, phone calls were prohibited with the exception of the ones we made every Sunday to our parents.

Having the power to make one phone call each was worth so much more than the monetary value of the card itself. It represented a tiny moment of freedom that loosened the noose from around our necks. We would have to be creative in when and where we chose to make our phone calls. We secretly arranged times for each of us and collaborated a security plan wherein two would be on guard while the other made their five-minute call. This plan was doomed to failure, as there were always eyes watching. We each made our respective calls and felt like they had gone unnoticed by those of authority. Unfortunately, this was not so.

A Soulful Awakening

I was in class when I heard Christina's name being called to the headmaster's office. Shortly after, I heard Katie's name being announced to do the same. My heart began to beat so quickly I felt like it was going to explode. I could not concentrate on the work before me, as the severity of the situation became clear to me. I became instantly angry with myself for taking such an unnecessary risk. I knew deep down in my core that this wrongdoing was all that the headmaster needed to bring an end to our dreams. I felt like I was drowning in fear as I heard my name being called over the loud speaker. My entire class looked down as I slowly dragged my body from the chair. It was as though they intuitively knew that my world was about to drastically change. My body reacted like it weighed a thousand pounds as it resisted my motion toward the dreaded headmaster's office.

Katie and Christina were sitting in the waiting room with their heads hung low as I walked past them and knocked on the door. The mere sight of our headmaster evoked deep-seeded feelings of fear, anger, resentment, loathing, and disappointment. I barely heard his words as I was questioned about the four-minute-and-thirty-two-second phone call that I had apparently made. I didn't attempt to make excuses, nor did I try to deny my actions. I was forthcoming and truthful as I replayed my part in the calling card. I felt and communicated remorse on a genuine level. I didn't feel that begging for forgiveness would have changed the course of disciplinary action, so I chose not to grovel for mercy. I did, however, offer a sincere apology that was bluntly denied acceptance.

Katie and Christina were both brought back into the room, and together we were suspended for two weeks. Upon our return to school, we would no longer be a part of the bike team or the cross-country ski team. We were strictly warned that any communication between us would result in instant expulsion.

Stephanie Banks

I do understand that we were wrong in our actions. We took something that didn't belong to us and we broke the rules of the school by making those phone calls. However, my parents and I believed that the punishment did not fit the crime. We didn't attempt to cover up our poor judgment or conceal our actions. When questioned, we spoke with honesty and integrity. It all seemed like a blur—like a dark storm had rolled into my world and the clouds that had formed blocked out the sun so intensely that I couldn't see any light at all.

With crushed hearts and feelings of anger and frustration, we boarded the train and immersed ourselves in our thoughts for the eight-hour train ride home to serve our two-week suspension.

I spent that time at home wallowing in sadness, dreading my return. My parents were very liberal and reminded me that I didn't have to go back if didn't want to. I had been focused on university as well as the teams, so I made a decision to finish my education at this school.

I dug deep inside to find my inner strength and recognized my fears as I sat in the backseat of my parent's car while driving back to school. I returned with an adjusted attitude on life to the best of my teenage abilities. I dreaded seeing the bike team heading to practices. I hoped to not hear any news on the provincials. It didn't take long before I learned that one of the staff kids had replaced me on both teams. I didn't blame her then, and I don't blame her now. She was young as well and felt like she didn't have a choice. I had assumed that the cross-country ski team would have dissolved, as we had qualified individually. Rather, we were informed that the team was still scheduled to go with new team members who were sent under our names and were told to lie about their identity. They signed in using our names, raced under our names, and probably lost under our names.

A Soulful Awakening

I now believe that the lesson of hypocrisy manifested itself to give me the opportunity to learn the meaning of this word firsthand. I could've read about it, learned how to spell it, done a thesis on it, but to experience the pain it was capable of creating—to feel it—would be the real lesson.

We continued school while under our own personal storm clouds and silently supported each other while waiting for the year to end. Christina was losing her mother to cancer during this time, so I was worried that this blow would knock her to the ground. Rather, I watched her in admiration as she diligently worked her way through the year.

We witnessed the new bike team struggle to jive, and I often wonder how it all went down. The team we had been a part of had developed a unique and tight bond. The removal of old team members and arrival of new ones at this point in training must have created a feeling of unrest.

Our days at the Christian collage came to an end. As that chapter closed, I was excited for the next one to begin. Katie and I decided to book a three-month trip to Europe prior to heading off to university. Christina was to head home to Smith Falls and be with her family while continuing her own education. We bid our farewells to our friends and foes as we graduated on a magnificent sunny day on the shores of the St. Lawrence River.

Years later, I received a lengthy newspaper article describing the unbecoming behavior of many of the staff members from my school and their affiliation with at least one cult. The school has now been closed since 2007 and is part of one of the largest class-action lawsuits in Canadian history, as hundreds of alumni came forward with allegations of abuse.

Stephanie Banks

Stef: Thank you for these messages and endless thought-provoking concepts. May we continue to be open to all the possibilities that lie before us. May we continue to swim in the sea of learning and understanding while soaking in the rays of patience, love, and happiness. I have been diving into my past and exploring my history at private school. I would love to receive a message on the subject of ego.

Ustro: *EGO: Enormous, Gigantic, Over the top!*

Ego is the bearer of negativity. It tries with endless determination to rule without regard for anyone. Ego is an endless circle of self-imposed obligations that serve only ego itself. Even the soul whose ego is directing is not benefiting from the wants of ego. The soul benefits and grows from needs being met but shrinks when the wants of ego are being met. Ego is directed by fear.

Under the umbrella of fear reside anguish, jealousy, negativity, resentment, judgment, manipulation, selfishness, and unkindness. Fear fears love. It fears love, because just like water is able to extinguish fire, love is able to extinguish fear and all else that fear represents. Fear appears to be strong and powerful, but in true universal reality, fear is easily disabled. When fear is disabled, so, too, is ego. Ego has many tools within its transparent toolbox. Usually, the first tool it will call upon is control. It will use whatever avenue it sees fit to use control within a situation.

This avenue may lead to a lie; it may be to use harsh and unkind words, which under the perfect circumstances will deflate another soul—hence, ego-gaining control. It may go so far as to use physical force. Another tool that may be called upon by ego is manipulation. Manipulation is defined as the use of words in an inappropriate manner with a self-serving objective in mind.

It is coercing another to partake in an activity that may appear beneficial to both parties but are not.

Manipulation creates a false sense of perception in another with the ultimate goal benefitting only the ego that it's manipulating. Manipulation creates an enormous karmic debt, and when recognized by either, the transmitter or receiver must be acknowledged and removed promptly. It is one of many untruths or creations that are not conducive at all to compassion of others. Ego will call upon emotional or physical abuse to gain control over another soul. There are usually no limitations with an ego when this tool is in use.

When you feel that another's ego is attempting to use this form of control on your soul, it's advised to remove yourself from the reach of the ego that is attempting to harm your soul, mind, and physical body. Call upon those you trust if you are unable to find a way out of this dark and endless cave.

Once ego has taken root in someone's soul in such a way, they must recognize, acknowledge, and learn new ways before change within will transpire. Oftentimes, this is a slow and arduous process; but with the intent to throw ego to the wind and diligence to embrace alternate ways of managing emotions, change will be created.

Ego will never entirely disappear from a person's being, as it is a necessary aspect of soul; it does, however, require constant reminders of its boundaries. Ego is like a high-maintenance vehicle that requires servicing frequently.

Stef: Many people seem to use the power of manipulation and control to get through life. Could you give us any insight into these unauthentic tools that seem to be prevalent in our time?

Ustro: *These tools are typically a result of money, but not always. Greed is a factor as well, and once manipulation is recognized, you will be able to smell it like a shark receiving a hint of blood in the ocean miles and miles away. When you do experience someone attempting to manipulate a situation, it is important to bear in mind your lesson of compassion and nonjudgment.*

Look at the circumstances and ask yourself what the underlying need is for the other or others involved. Are they desperate to achieve certain results because they perhaps fear the outcome? This is usually the case; if so, this would be your cue to exemplify compassion, as you will recognize the power of fear. A soulful response would be to shine a new light on the incident or situation. This would be an ideal time to practice with communication skills and make a heartfelt attempt to acknowledge the person's needs and the value that you place on those needs while providing some insight in a more positive and productive approach.

This would simply be a request for honesty in light of what is being requested of you. For example, you have a friend who really needs to borrow something of value from you. The approach taken by your friend simply seems controlling in nature, and you feel that you would be slightly used if you were to accept the request. First, do not take this personally, as it is not a reflection of you or your personal journey. If you feel the need to accommodate your friend, simply express your concern with how the request was presented, and then either accept the request or do not. Accept your decision, knowing that you have based this decision purely on the other's needs and also your need to feel appreciated and respected.

Although you are learning not to take things personally, we all need to feel respect from another. Respect and love are roommates and should always cohabitate in unison. Without one, the other does not truly exist. For some, this will be a new concept, simply because the art of love and loving has been buried. Anything that has been buried is retrievable, as long as the hands that are digging really do feel the need to find what they are looking for. We all need to feel loved and respected; it is an integral aspect of being a human being. If respect for others is lacking, then a close-up view of self-respect is encouraged.

How can we possibly respect others if self-respect is lacking? The same is true for the counterpart of respect: love. How can one possibly feel and show love for another in the pure sense if one does not feel pure and unconditional love for themselves? This is why reflection inwardly is essential to our learning. Once we are in a place of inner strength and understanding, we will be able to share ourselves freely without demands in return. There should never be an anticipated outcome when dealing with other souls. Requests can be made as long as expectations do not exist. There will always be an alternate route that will be available to you; eventually, what you seek will find you.

Oftentimes, the things we are in need of lie right before us, but the mind complicates matters and closes doors that would otherwise be open for exploration. Keep everything clear and concise; ask the universe to guide you on your search. Stay focused and remain diligent while staying on your own track. The objective here is to respect the lanes of others and not to barge or push them to the side while you continue on your way. Feel free to make a pass as long as it is done so in a clean manner—preferably with love left in the dust.

Stef: There have been many times throughout my life when I have felt judged by others. This was especially apparent while attending boarding school. Does anyone have anything they would like to say in regards to judgment and criticism?

Stephanie Banks

Abel: *I am in the air we breathe, the water we drink, the rivers and the sky above. When we universally give thanks, we will be blessed with pure love.*

As a parent, there have been and will be more moments in time when we allow our own will to overshadow the will of our children. They are on their own trail of discovery, and we need to trust in them completely. They, as well as ourselves, have predetermined their path that will lead them to many intersections, which will require turns to be made. The decisions made at these times will reflect their inner judgment, based on lessons learned both here in this lifetime and many others.

Judgment is not real. It is an imaginary tool created by ego and power, and it has been bred into our human lives. It takes strength, self-control, and diligence to overcome the want to judge. Remember, we are all from the same roots system. When judgment is passed onto someone or something, it stings us as well. Repel the feeling to judge. It is simply a bad habit that needs to be broken. We seem to gain false personal satisfaction from this until we realize the negative effects.

Remember, judgment does not have a place in the understanding of fellow souls; we are all one and need to be respected as such. Open your heart's pathway to a larger and richer life and you will feel and experience more than you can imagine. You will then have the capacity to share your new realizations, which, in turn, will bring contentment to all.

Sherman H. Harlow: *Everything will play out as the author has designed it to do. We are our own authors, creators of our own tales, editors, and illustrators, not to mention critics. Criticism, along with power and manipulation, are false perceptions of something real. Here is what I mean by that: for the most part,* we live our lives externally. Doing tasks that we believe will make us better people based on how other people perceive how we accomplish those tasks. Will we do them well enough to meet their standards, or will we be criticized negatively? Criticism essentially is judgment. Judgment is also false, not real. They are all tools that the human mind—intellect—has created in order to attempt to cope with fear. I will leave that for now. Those are difficult concepts to grasp and translate.

Chapter 7
Hello and Good-bye

"Life is beauty, admire it.
Life is a dream, realize it.
Life is a challenge, meet it.
Life is a game, play it.
Life is a song, sing it.
Life is an adventure, dare it.
Life is precious, do not destroy it."
—Mother Theresa

Katie and I traveled to Europe together as planned, and upon our return to Canada, we parted ways to embark on our university careers. During the first year, Katie and I lost touch due to a disagreement. The disagreement was a silly one, just as most are. Our campuses were located in different cities a few hours apart. I expected Katie to come visit me, and she expected me to visit her.

As I look back with a clearer understanding of life, I find it amazing how expectations have a similar effect on humans as toxicity does. They both slowly and silently disperse into our systems destroying all the good along the way. With expectations, we invalidate clear thinking and good intentions. Both become clouded by the wants

A Soulful Awakening

of the ego. The ego feels the urgency to have its wants met by others while ignoring the needs of others.

Neither Katie nor I made the trip to see the other; this would mark the beginning of two years of silence. We didn't talk to one another during this time due to our stubbornness and unwillingness to put our egos aside. Our parents were distraught about our friendship breakup, but there was nothing they could say or do to change our minds.

Partway through the first year of university, my knee succumbed to multiple injuries that set me in a full leg brace for many months. With my sights set on a degree in kinesiology, my dreams once again began to unravel simultaneously to the cartilage in my knee. I had a difficult time simply getting myself dressed, let alone maneuvering from one class to the next.

The University of Western Ontario is approximately the same population as my hometown, and the buildings are spread across many kilometers. The ability to learn amongst so many students required arriving to class early enough to score a good seat. The smallest class I had enrolled in was no less than five hundred people. Most of my professors at university chose not to wear a microphone, so hearing the lectures was a challenge for those seated toward the back of the lecture halls. My knee prevented me from running to and from classes, so I quickly realized that not only was my knee going to damage my athletic endeavors, but it was also going to have a negative effect on my schooling.

I managed to complete my first year with mediocre grades and a knee that functioned well enough to take me out West to work for the summer. I contemplated my options in regards to my education, and it became clear to me that the kinesiology program would not be conducive for someone such as myself who suffered from a debilitating knee.

I decided to take some time off school; therefore, Lake Louise Alberta became my home for the next three years, alongside my brother but away from my mother. The distance between my mom and myself was difficult for us both, as it felt like the umbilical cord was still attached.

I missed Katie as well but I was holding on tight to my position of feeling right. I traveled to Hong Kong, Australia, New Zealand, Fiji, and Hawaii during this time of my life. As much as I longed to share my experiences with Katie, I chose not to. I wrote cards and letters to my other friends and family but not Katie, who had been my best mate for ten years.

The spring of 1994 arrived and with it came a profound universal experience. I had just returned to Lake Louise after a six-month trip abroad, and I was scheduled to work that evening. My employer and brother, who was the manager at the time, had graciously held my position as I traveled, with the understanding that I would return to work in April.

As I made my way to work, I passed by a payphone and felt an uncontrollable urgency to call my mother, whom I had just spoken to the day before. I followed my intuition and called my mom, and we had a great conversation. There was nothing unusual about our chat. We were both happy and healthy, yet as I hung up the phone, my body collapsed to the floor and I began to sob uncontrollably. My brother was the first to come upon me and attempted to help me understand why I was so upset. I didn't know why I was feeling this way, but I knew with certainty that I needed to go home to Stratford. I didn't have any money and I had made a commitment to work, yet I was determined to get home. With a helping hand and no questions asked, my boss kindly drove me to the Calgary Airport and bought my ticket home that evening.

As I sat on the plane, my mind kept returning to Katie. Memories of our times together flashed before me like a movie within my mind. Feelings of love for her and our friendship exploded within me like fireworks lighting up my mind's eye. I understand now in hindsight that the universe was playing its part in reconciling our differences before that opportunity was lost. At the time, my mind swirled with anticipation of calling her the minute I disembarked the plane.

My mother greeted me at the airport with hugs and kisses. I was elated to be held in her arms, yet I longed to feel Katie's embrace. I didn't have a current phone number for her, as we had not spoken in years. As it was approaching midnight, my mother suggested that I wait until the morning to call her parents.

That night as I lay in bed, I wrestled around with pillows, blankets, and thoughts as the seconds ticked by at an irritatingly sluggish pace. Second by second, I counted to 9:00 a.m. before frantically dialing her parent's number. Katie's mom answered and was ecstatic to hear my voice. She did not waste time with idle chitchat as she filled me in on Katie's whereabouts.

She had left the day before I traveled home on a multiple-day rafting trip down the Ottawa River. I would be in Stratford for seven days, and Katie was scheduled to call her parents from Ottawa the day before I was to be returning back to Lake Louise. There was no way of reaching her until then, so I began counting the seconds once again. I waited and waited and waited. I paced around my mother's house, testing her patience. The phone finally sang its wonderful tune, and I heard Katie's voice on the other end. It was 5:30 p.m. the night before I was to fly back out west. Katie and I made plans to meet at 6:00 p.m. at our old-time hangout, Bentley's.

It was a magical reunion and one that I will always cherish. Hours passed without notice as we exchanged stories while oblivious to the world around us. We made vows to one another that placed honor on our friendship as opposed to our immature Egos. Eventually, we were asked to settle up the bill for our last supper.

As we departed through the back door, Katie grabbed her bike. We hugged each other with an unprecedented feeling of love. We made promises to remain connected and to visit each other without expectation. As she mounted her bike and peddled away, I turned in the opposite direction and took a few sad steps. The world around me seemed to become peacefully quiet and slow. It was as though time in that space had stopped. In that unearthly magical moment, I felt as though we had melted into a realm that was full of unconditional love and peace. The silence and calm that embedded itself into my soul blessed me with an insight to clarity.

Through the haze I heard my name as it echoed through the blissful air. Without hesitation I pivoted, just as I did when we played basketball and she was calling for a pass. Rather than passing a ball, she blew me a kiss. I felt her entire energy engulf my being as she drifted quietly and eloquently off into the distance. My eyes squinted as they followed her outline into the darkness. I didn't want that moment to end. I wanted to hold it there and never let go, but the universe gracefully returned me back to the reality I was more familiar with.

I took the long way home that night as I attempted to gather my thoughts and sift through the assortment of emotions that flooded my system. I replayed our conversations over and over in my mind, as if to fossilize them into the memory bank of my soul for eternity. We had been through so much together, and the thought of parting ways once again instigated a sense of anxiety and sadness. I still had so much to say and so many stories left untold.

The following morning, my mother drove me back to the airport, where we embraced and said good-bye. I had been so absorbed in my thoughts of Katie throughout the week that I was beginning to feel regretful for not using the time I had to enjoy each moment with my mother.

CHAPTER 8

Denial and Acceptance

"It takes no more time to see
the good side of life than to see the bad."
—Jimmy Buffet

I quickly settled back into the routine of Lake Louise. During my first week back from Ontario, I repaid my boss for the airline ticket and began a letter to Katie expressing my happiness for both our reunion and our friendship. After a long night of work, I settled into the warmth of my bed, picked up the unfinished letter, and again began to write. I wrote a few sentences before my eyelids closed, and I drifted off to sleep.

Dreamland is a wonderfully magical place to visit each night. It reminds me of opening a gift. You don't know what's inside until you take a peek. Dreams are like that initial peek—you see a fragment of the whole picture. That fragment stirs the imagination that seems to lie dormant during the day and awakens to creativity during sleep. I believe dreamland and the awakened state are two parallel coexisting realms. During sleep, the curtain rises, allowing for creative exploration and connections to flow freely, unobstructed by conscious thought. While in dreamland,

A Soulful Awakening

we are more in tune with our higher selves and the collective consciousness of all.

My body flew off the bed in a heap of confusion as I stumbled blindly half-asleep to the ringing of the phone downstairs. I fumbled with the receiver while my eyes focused on the numbers on the stove. It was just after 5 a.m. I felt a sudden pang in my gut as I lifted the phone. I instantly knew that something was not right. That feeling in my gut that my mom spoke so highly of was warning me to take a deep breath and hold on tight. I wanted to quietly place the receiver back in its home and return to the safety of my bed. I didn't want to acknowledge the voice I heard saying my name as I gripped the phone tightly to my ear. I had been immersed in a dream before being so rudely awakened. Through the fog of the moment, I kept hearing the words, "St Joseph's." My mind would then return to my mother's voice as she called my name, "Nini". My mother's pet name for me was Nini, and I didn't know the meaning of St. Joseph's, as it was merely a word running through my head at that point.

Finally, I managed to utter, "Hello?" I felt my body slide down the kitchen wall as my legs gave way to the emotional tidal wave as it breached the floodgates within. My mind swirled as it digested the words, "Katie was killed last night." Katie had died in a tragic car crash as I slept with her un-mailed letter safely tucked under my arms. That letter would never be mailed, and she would never have the opportunity to read it.

"St Joseph's, St Joseph's, St Joseph's." These were the words I heard again and again as I gathered together a travel bag. I had said hello to Katie fewer than two weeks ago, and now I would be flying home to say good-bye. I would collapse for moments at a time while I witnessed new fears creep into my sacred space. My soul felt like it was suspended in frigid water through a tiny hole beneath a thick layer of ice. How would I ever find my way back up to the surface? How would I continue life without my best friend?

A flight had been booked, and arrangements had been made to get me to the airport that morning. Once I was settled into my seat, I immediately turned my thoughts to writing in my journal. I have always believed that writing in any form is therapeutic to the soul. I pulled out two markers, red and black, along with my journal that I had stuffed hastily into my bag. I began to write words of anger, frustration, and sadness. I drew pictures, wrote poems, and doodled Katie's name in various ways as I released the emotions that would otherwise have debilitated me entirely. I often wonder what the person who was sitting beside me was thinking as I created profanities in bubble letters attached to the word *why*. Why did this happen to Katie? Why my best friend? Why now? These are questions that all of us ask in times such as these.

I felt shattered and un-repairable. I felt like an old, discarded vehicle that had been waiting to be crushed at the junkyard. Darkness had made her debut yet again. She had settled into recession since my private school experience as I traveled the world living a carefree life. But here she was once again, reminding me that life on earth could present itself as painful and cruel from time to time. Darkness and I had become intimate companions during my days at school, but lightness and I were familiar with one another as well. Lightness is entrenched deep within our souls, and when darkness creeps in, we must challenge it. This can be a tremendously difficult duo, but with faith and trust, it is one worth fighting.

In between profanities on the pages of my journal, I wrote wonderful words of love. The story of Katie and I reminded me of a tragic love story. I could feel lightness encouraging me to focus on the love that brought light to our lives. This battle would not be quick and easy, but eventually the light within me would capture the flag and raise it high for all to see.

It seemed like déjà vu as my mother greeted me at the airport. We collapsed into each other's arms as we made our way blindly through the hoards of seemly happy people. It's strange how the sight of joyful people can be sickening when we are feeling so distraught. Aside from the relentless voice in my head regurgitating the word *St. Joseph's*, we drove home to Stratford in silence. The dream from the night before replayed in my mind over and over. I had been standing in an old, large building by myself. I gazed in awe at the details of this magnificent structure, but just like most dreams, I couldn't recall those details. As I sat remembering the dream I quietly asked my mother where Katie's funeral would be held, but she didn't know.

Later that afternoon, I met Katie's boyfriend for the first time. She had spent most of our last visit describing his every detail, so I felt as though we were long-lost friends. We hugged while silently acknowledging our mutual love for our friend. As I interacted with Katie's family later that afternoon, it became clear to me where Katie drawn her strength from while we were teenagers. Her parents, two brothers, and sister all exhibited the same inner strength that Katie carried with her always. I stood in their living room remembering all the times Katie and I had stood there together. I felt her presence and decided to honor her by tapping into the strength and love that I felt in that room at that time.

Katie's parents kindly asked if I would prepare and deliver the eulogy for the funeral. I didn't know what a eulogy was, but I knew that it sounded like an honor I couldn't refuse. As they described the meaning of *eulogy*, fear and anxiety came out to play like bullies lurking on the playground, waiting to attack my confidence. I had loathed public speaking on any level, so the thought of delivering a speech to hundreds of mourning people was overwhelming. I pondered revoking my acceptance of this honor, but when fear rears its ugly face, courage rises to the occasion. Rather than caving to fear, I looked to Sean and my inner strength for support. Together, he and I would give the eulogy of her lifetime.

I spent the next few days leading up to Katie's funeral mustering together words that I felt were fitting for this celebration of life. Just as we had done many times before, I sat beneath the old willow tree behind our public high school. Its long, droopy branches gave me a sense of protectiveness as I leaned against its sturdy trunk for support. A bench would later be placed in this spot in remembrance of her beautiful life.

The night before the funeral, we gathered in a small but quaint funeral home for her wake. The meaning of this gathering was to allow for close family and friends to share a quiet moment with Katie's body. As much as I craved time with her, I wasn't prepared for the onslaught of emotions that came over me as I approached the open casket. Her body lay lifeless with her arms folded across her chest. I reached out in desperation to feel her warmth but was startled by the stiffness and coldness of her hand. Her motionless body was covered beautifully in the dress that she wore during our graduation at private school. Memories of that day of liberation engulfed me as I grasped her hand, not wanting to let go. I couldn't find words to share with her but placed a tiger lily on her chest as a symbol of our friendship.

I stood grounded by her energy that I knew was still very much alive. I reminded myself that this was simply her body, a vehicle that she had chosen to maneuver herself through this lifetime. I felt her spirit rise up inside me as I backed away from her side. Her soul lingered in that room consoling us.

As we departed the funeral home, her parents asked that Sean and I meet them at St. Joseph's church the next morning. I squinted my eyes as if I had been awakened once again from the dream I had the night Katie died. The building I had dreamed about would be the church where I would give her eulogy in honor of her time on earth.

Once again, I was reminded of the complexity of life and all that it encompasses. I was mystified knowing that I had experienced this church prior to being informed of my friend's death, or had I known on a deeper more connected level through dreaming? Had I been there with her in spirit as she transitioned from this world to the next? Although I didn't have definitive answers to these questions, I felt a sense of peace simply by pondering them. My mother had experienced these sorts of synchronicities through dreaming numerous times throughout her life, so she didn't seem as surprised as I did. To her, these profound experiences were just as much a part of life as breathing.

I opted to walk home that night after the wake, and in doing so, I found myself standing humbly before the steps of St. Joseph's church. I marveled at its architecture and its overall beauty. The old yellow bricks and stained glass windows beckoned me to approach. My hands grasped the oversized, wooden door handle as I gave it a tug, but to my disappointment, it was locked. My legs took me to the back of the building and led me directly to an open door. I entered tentatively as though I was a trespasser. There was just enough light to find my way through to the chapel. I felt like I had been here before, and I was retracing my footsteps.

As I entered the main chapel area, my eyes focused on the intricacy of the stained glass windows. As my eyes drifted around the enormous room, I envisioned how I would feel the next day when the wooden pews would be full of guests paying their respect for Katie. I made my way to the altar and stood with Jesus hanging on a cross behind me. I visualized my speech being delivered flawlessly. I asked the universe to help me find the strength I needed to get through the next day. The similarity between that moment in the church and my dream could not be overlooked. We are bound to a higher consciousness at all times.

The following day inevitably arrived. I sat in the front row of the church alongside Katie's family facing the priest as others filed in behind us taking their seats. Sean held my hand as I clenched the eulogy in the other. When the time came, we approached the altar. As we stood there, I took a brief moment to look around and absorb the energy of the room. My eyes returned to the stained glass windows, and from there, I found the courage to speak.

My voice trembled, my body ached, but my heart was open. As I delivered her eulogy, I realized that life for all of us would continue. I had a moment of clarity as I stood before hundreds of people. We don't travel through life alone; we are here to guide, assist, and protect each other through the process. I felt a deep sense of love surround me as I was engulfed in a unified love for Katie.

I returned to Lake Louise feeling as though I had transformed into an adult overnight. I looked at life through a much clearer lens. Through death we come to realize the preciousness of life. We appreciate time more and develop a deeper respect for our usage of that time. Although it took many years before I felt Katie's presence through my other senses, I did know on some level of my being that she was there with me when I asked her to be. I spent countless hours after her death wandering through the woods, hiking mountains, and sitting by the waters edge of the Bow River. There were moments when I found myself screaming to the universe in anger and sadness. There were moments when I allowed myself to surrender to the simple facts of life. I found solace in music and nature when nothing else seemed to penetrate me in a peaceful manner.

For those of you who have experienced death, I commend you for digging deep as you find your inner light within the darkness of the shadows. I encourage you to empower yourself through acceptance of death as a necessary aspect of our current reality while embracing the fact that death of physical life is a rebirth of the soul. Once we acknowledge this truth, we can live with it in our hearts. We will open the door to exploration of other realms and possibilities that are within our reach. Reach out to those you feel you have lost, and you will see that they are not lost at all; they are right here with us in one form or another. Ask for their guidance and their protection, and you will feel their love.

The first message I received from Katie was many years after her death as I awakened to the spiritual world after the bike crash. I specifically asked if she was there, and if so, could she deliver a message? So she did. It is really that simple. Ask, and you shall receive.

Stef: Today is your birthday, Katie. I miss you all the time even if there are days that go by without a thought of you or us together. Are you there, and if so, would you mind giving us a message? From time to time, we as humans engage in disagreements, as you know. Afterward, we feel sad and disappointed in our own behavior and the behavior of others. How do we best manage these scenarios when they occur?

Katie: *You are so lovely and sweet. Bittersweet at times too. Be more cautious with your words and remember to plan not to react. There are recurring themes, as you are witnessing throughout these messages. This is a big one and goes for us all. Do not be hard on yourself. Remember, life is strictly about learning, not about perfecting all our lessons in one given step. Remember also: baby steps pave the way to enlightenment.*

There will always be times of discourse and disagreement, but without these challenging times, how would we learn? Look upon your quarrels with an open mind into another perspective and allow all feelings of ego to step aside. Ask compassion, love, and peace to step forward and allow your soul to acknowledge any feelings of anger that may have emerged during the quarrel.

Once these emotions have been recognized and acknowledged, ask for forgiveness from yourself. Before asking for forgiveness from others, we must first ask for forgiveness from ourselves, because we must only answer to our own inner self. We are on our own journeys, and it is difficult to escape the feeling of guilt. Guilt is a feeling very much like fear; it can breed like rabbits. There is no need to ever feel guilt if we simply ask our own inner self for forgiveness and understanding. With this asking of forgiveness, we must also consciously set a new intention to act in a loving and compassionate manner in every capacity of life.

If we continually set this intention, we will move in the direction of ascension. With denial of our own actions, healthy or otherwise, we are only denying ourselves of our own evolution. Wandering aimlessly without regard for our thoughts, words, or actions will take us to the land of continual absence of spiritual growth. This will feel like a forest with no way out. No shining ray of sunshine to guide us to everlasting love.

Good-bye ego. Hello, love.

Stef: Does anyone have a message to contribute today on the subject of expectations? So many times expectations have caused me grief and anguish; I'm sure we all suffer from this every now and then.

Solomon: *We cannot have expectations of either others or ourselves. Expectations are an extension of control and greed, an extension of fear. If we feel that we have created expectations of either others or ourselves, we need to figure out why we have put these quiet little demands into play. Once we understand why we made that move, we must learn to remove them from the field of life. Expectations will lead to anger, guilt, jealousy, and pain.*

Stef: It is 5:00 a.m., and while the sky remains dark, the light inside me is shining bright. I woke with a strong feeling that I was learning throughout my sleep; however, I am unable to recall what the lesson or lessons were. I am hopeful that someone will be able to give us some insight into how our dreams influence our awake time and also the best way to help us remember events that go on through our night time slumber. Is there anyone who would like to contribute today?

Ruby: *Talk to me, child. I am open. I am free. Soaring in the wind, rising in the sun, floating on the water, and weathering all the storms that you see through your eyes.*

We travel through many realms at different times, recognizing the difference while experiencing the similarities of these realms is a challenge at first. Our nighttime slumber, as you so eloquently termed it, is simply a peaceful time of reflection and creativity that is accompanied by the rejuvenation of the physical body. This is a time for the body to recoup from the daily activities and stresses. *A time for old and damaged cells to be replaced with new, energized cells—a time for the body and all of its wonderful components to slow down and rest peacefully.*

When the body and mind rest, so, too, does the soul. This quiet time is essential for all aspects of your living self. We tend to view this rest period as a time in reality that we are no longer awake, when in actuality, we are just as awake as we are throughout the day. The same principle is true for times of meditation and relaxation. When we enable ourselves to rest on any level, we are awakened to other realms and possibilities that we may otherwise miss. Dreams are another reality that offer insight and clarity and demonstrate an alternate view for us to explore. There are many different ways of interpreting situations or circumstances.

Through our dreams, we experience the innate ability to stray from interpreting through the means of our minds and look at experiences through the eye of our soul. We are more in tune with our inner selves during times of rest, and therefore, are able to interpret intuitively rather than through the use of knowledge and the laws of society. As you awaken in the spiritual sense, you will experience a shift in your sleep. Your dreams will begin to feel more like a continuation of your daily lessons rather than a movie being played simply for your enjoyment. You will feel more rejuvenated and ready to greet the dawn after a night's sleep ensued with spiritual growth. Even when you feel that you may have forgotten what you experienced, remember that all lessons and wisdom shared are engraved in your soul and you will find a way of exposing that truth through your consciousness.

For some, taking notes as you awaken when your mind is still unobstructed by thought provides an opportunity to bring clarity and remembrance to their night. Try meditating as you fall into your slumber and ask the universe to aid you on your night's journey as well as your ability to consciously recall the events that transpire throughout your sleep. Ask for healing both within your physical and non-physical self. Prior to slumber is an opportune moment in time to ask yourself, your higher self, for forgiveness if this is necessary.

Ask for continued compassion to flow through your being as you journey through life. Give gratitude for all that you feel grateful for. Once you are in a place of calmness, let all thoughts go and allow another reality to unfold as you rest. There is a great deal of pleasure to be experienced through sleep. Enjoy this time of tranquility.

Stef: Thank you, Ruby. Could someone please give us another perspective on death, as we know it here on earth?

Solomon: *I am everywhere, everything. Ask, and you shall receive. I fly with the eagles and play with your dogs. I am particles; I am whispers; I am all that you ask me to be. You can now call on me when you see fit. I will engulf you in my veil of energy as often as you like. I may not always answer your prayers as you may wish, but you have lessons to learn that you have specifically chosen. I am merely a character in your book of life on earth. My role is to protect. I protect you as you have predetermined. If your time has not come to leave earth and danger sets in, I step in and ease the pain.*

Death on earth is a difficult—the most difficult—lesson to comprehend, at least for those left behind to pick up the pieces of their puzzle disturbed. Once humans return to their roots, death will not be such an insurmountable hill to climb. We will see death for all that it truly is: a transition in time and space. A fixed moment dictated by circumstance created by our higher selves. As we together begin to truly believe in the universe as a whole, with the understanding that the soul does not die or ever disappear, we will inevitably grasp the meaning, the purpose, and the physics that go along with death. Death of the physical body is essential for the rebirth of the soul.

Dianne: *Rise above pain, anger, and even despair. At times, those we love, must soar beyond our regular grasp, but remember that they are forever here. Love yourself wholly and completely without regret. I breathe the air you breathe. I dream the same dreams, as our souls are bound at their roots. Never let go of hope and faith. Remember: resilience is the key to longevity, forever is nothing, and nothing is forever.*

I am free. I am happy. Fly beyond your wildest dreams, and you will soar to heights unimaginable. I loved my life, and love it still. I will continue to learn here in this realm until I see fit to return. Return, I will, as I have much to learn. I will enjoy this moment here for now, as it is really quite lovely, the epitome of tranquility and calm. I am of assistance here. You are all set on a journey that only you are able to create. Use your inner strength to set your course and aid in your journey to places yet seen. Find a passion—something that sets your soul free, something that you wake thinking about and something that you fall asleep dreaming about.

Continue to move through life on earth recognizing the beauty and brilliance of it all. Continue to value and respect all life and each breath taken. Your life is a lesson, and learning you must do. Spread all the peace that you hold in your heart; it is replenishable. Simply ask for more when you wish. Enjoy your quiet time; it is nourishing for both your physical body and your soul.

Complete faith in the unknown, lack of concern for tomorrow, and undivided attention on today will bring you to a place of pure joy. Look into the eyes of those with whom you speak. Listen with care and understanding. Watch the world pass by yours without comment or judgment. Judgment does not exist here, nor does hate or anger—simply love and understanding. Help to spread both of these, as you are quite capable of doing.

There is so much more, so much more. We are blessed, truly blessed. Do not be wasteful with your time or resources; both are precious and need to be placed in a temple. Ask the universe to replenish your energy when you are feeling in need. It will flow continuously and effortlessly, but you need to make a conscious effort in this regard. Like all lessons, we must first recognize what the lesson is, and then understand how to achieve brilliance in that lesson and apply the energy required.

Look for me in the stars, the moon, the trees, their needles and leaves. Feel me as you breathe. We together are free and strong. We are love; we are part of a divine universe.

The day before my crash in Whistler.

Dawson and I outside Whistler Emergency.

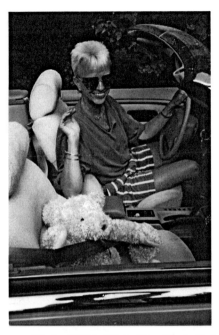

My mom Linda (1994–95) in Stratford, Ontario.

My father Steve, Spence, and I at our first meeting since 1974 in Hamilton, Ontario.

Me in front of my boarding school in grade 11.

Katie and I in Europe after graduation at a garbage bag party.

Katie and I in Venice. I had just turned nineteen.

Katie Kenny.

Katie's memorial bench in Stratford, Ontario.

Grandpa Harold.

The church that held the evangelist.

CHAPTER 9

Bonnie's Story

"People will forget what you've said,
people will forget what you did
but people will never forget how you made them feel."
—Maya Angelou

The air was cool that day; it was as though the chill had already set into my world. I may have been the only one to feel it, but it was very much real to me. As I answered the phone and heard my mother's best friend on the other end, the chill embedded deeper into my twenty-four-year-old bones as she informed me of my mother's terminal illness. Just yesterday, I had been hiking along the shoreline of Dallas drive in Victoria, BC, with the warmth of tranquility surrounding me as I ventured through my days carefree and void of any real responsibility.

Today, those days would fade into a distant memory. I should have taken more time to appreciate those days of ease, but until something is gone, we have a tendency to believe that these special moments are limitless. Why do we think this way as humans? Is it a way of self-preservation? Is it our way of avoiding our deepest fears? Maybe it is from a lack of awareness of what is truly important and what is not. Either way, I have now come to realize how precious and irreplaceable every moment in time truly is.

As I looked around at what had become my home, I accepted that this was not my home anymore. I was needed and must pack what few items I valued enough to take with me to my mother's home in Stratford. My mom, had been quite ill for some time. I had not been privy to this information, as I believe our mother didn't wish to burden us with such news. The time had come when my brother and I needed to be informed about the state of our mother's health and make some decisions. There is a period of time after that phone call that remains blank to me, tucked away in a deep compartment of my memory bank that I have yet to access. I cannot recall booking a flight or actually being on a plane, for that matter. I cannot remember going to work during those days of transition. I cannot remember any conversations with my brother or anyone else regarding the circumstances. I do recall one brief chat with my boyfriend of the time regarding the change in direction of my life. I told him that I was glad to have met him and that I had enjoyed our brief time together, but my presence was required by my mother's side. I also have a vivid recollection of one incident that I rarely speak of.

My brother had bought me an old sea captain's trunk to pack my belongings. Once I had the trunk packed, he would have it shipped to Ontario. At the time, we were living together with my brother's girlfriend and another couple, Jack and Bonnie. I had failed to find any connection with Bonnie; however, we had been living amicably together. There was an aspect of her personality that I felt threatened by, but I couldn't figure out what that was. This was simply an intuitive feeling and nothing more.

It was a drizzly gray day as I rode my bike home from work to finish the packing I had begun the previous night. I would be leaving Victoria in less than a week and needed to have my trunk shipped as soon as possible. I parked my bike and was greeted by Bonnie and Jack as I entered our house; they seemed suspiciously kind as we passed idle remarks about the day.

Once in my bedroom, I opened my trunk, which I thought I had left open. I instinctively began to unpack everything that I had already packed. I didn't know what I was looking for; I simply felt an urgency to dig through my few life's possessions. It took but only a few minutes to account for numerous missing articles of clothing and a pair of hippie sticks that I had made.

My heart began to pump blood throughout my body with such velocity that I felt as though my veins would explode. Could it be true that my roommates would steal from me, especially in such difficult times? My mind swirled with questions, so I decided to direct those questions to the supposed culprits. En route to the living room, I took a detour into Bonnie's bedroom and marched directly to her own trunk, which was also being packed, as they, too, had plans to move. Before Bonnie had a chance to stop my search, I had pulled numerous items that belonged to me from the depth of her things. As she watched from her doorway, I witnessed lightning strike from behind her eyes as the thunder raged within her being.

As I witnessed this storm brewing, I gathered my belongings, dodged past her, and bolted back to the safety of my own room. My footsteps were followed by an entourage of threats and verbal abuse as she pounded on my door like a lion being held captive. My heart was pounding violently. I looked to my window as a possible route to escape this angry tyrant but decided that the fall would be too painful. I didn't have a phone to call for help, and no one would be home for hours. As the verbal threats continued from outside my door, I hid beneath my blankets like a horrified child hiding from the boogie monster. As the yelling and screaming continued, I felt my body succumb to a complete depletion of strength and energy. I began to sob uncontrollably until I realized that the racket had disappeared. As I lay huddled underneath my security blanket savoring the silence of the moment, sleep came over me like a heavy fog stretching across a lake. My eyes became heavy as I allowed myself to drift away from this place of turmoil.

This blissful state came to an abrupt end when I awoke to my door being brought down by the force of mighty Bonnie. As her brutish body and flailing blonde hair came bounding across my room, I didn't have the time or the strength to ward off this venomous creature. A struggle began as this person with such pent-up anger, who was about to release it all, enveloped me. I called upon all my inner forces as I desperately tried to untangle myself from this octopus. I found that my arms and legs were tied down firmly by the weight of her body and knees. I gasped for breath as her forearm pressed unforgiving across my neck. The lightning that had struck within her had begun a fire that was blazing out of control. I tried once again to squirm my way out of her grip, but any strength I had was now completely gone. I felt my cheeks burning as the blood flow was being cut off. Through the haze, I could hear the distant pleas from Jack for Bonnie to get off of me. As darkness felt like it was settling in, I began to feel a lightness sweep over me as I felt Bonnie's body being forcefully yanked from mine. I inhaled deeply and took a desperate breath as my airways became unrestricted. The door slammed behind them as my body collapsed in fear.

The following day, I left without a word and spent the next six days with my boyfriend. This was my good-bye from my roommates as I departed Victoria and began the next phase of my life.

As I recalled this event over the years that followed, I recognized how my own reactions added fuel to the fire. I acknowledged how I enabled the situation to flourish out of control rather than look for ways to deflate an already-inflated situation. I chose to react as opposed to respond, putting myself in harm's way.

The story of Bonnie and how I was treated is an example of how human beings are capable of treating each other poorly, without the recognition that we are all one. We disregard the truth that our roots are bound and tied together throughout eternity. Forgetting the simple fact that when we choose to mistreat a fellow soul, we are, in turn, mistreating our own soul and all that is. The Bonnie story exemplifies buried emotions surfacing in the form of fear represented by anger and dominance. We have all experienced this type of mistreatment in one way or another at some point in our lives. The lesson here is to recognize the potential harm that fear is able to create and to learn to diffuse strenuous situations before they erupt. It's important to respond to all circumstances in a soulful manner as opposed to reacting to an overflow of emotions, acting through compassion, and understanding rather than through the eyes of fear.

Stef: Taking things personally, this is a difficult lesson for many. To truly refrain from taking the actions of others personally, what lessons do we need to focus on?

Solomon: *Look at the animal kingdom for the answers here. Animals do not take offense. Even when facing the eyes of their predator, they do not judge the other; each is surviving in a unison world—each needing food, water, shelter, and love. Animals have an instinctual respect for one another. Humans have the difficult challenge of setting emotions aside. Animals instinctively deal with circumstances as they arise; there is no such thing as beating around the bush.*

Communication is the key to avoiding feeling hurt by others. Set your standards through the eyes of compassion and express yourself with love, respect, and clarity for both yourself and those with whom you are conversing. There will be progression combined with regression, be patient and a positive outcome will be achieved.

Stef: The story of Bonnie and I is one that I feel could have been avoided in so many ways. The pain that we are able to create on our planet is extremely detrimental to our health and well-being on so many levels. Is there a message for me to transmit today that highlights these topics?

Author unknown: *The creation of chaos magnifies the lessons we are in need of learning. We do the best we can with the lessons we have learned, the lessons still underway, and the tools we have gathered along the way.*

Pain is created by us and directed unto others and ourselves. Every action that originates from our emotions rather than our spirit inevitably becomes a drain on our soul—devitalizing, compromising, and challenging in a way that will call out a battle. Simply using the word battle *in explanation brings forth a feeling of shame and inadequacy.*

The energy required to battle is increasingly immense. Increasing because of the state of denial that most of the planet chooses to live—denial of the truth, denial of more, denial of our raw, authentic beings that are cocooned within a web of destruction; destruction on a spiritual level, and destruction on a physical level. As the world, or humans, continue to insist on living in such an unharmonious manner, destruction unfolds. A negative thought, unjust words, or unfavorable actions against any species that shares our space produces a new scar that will take time and energy to heal. Healing has begun and is underway. Healing of the heart, healing of the soul, healing of our physical bodies, healing of our mental well-being. Through chaos comes confusion, through confusion comes judgment, through judgment comes anger, and eventually hate.

As a well is about to run dry, we turn off the pump in order to allow the reservoir to replenish; so, too, is the need to turn off the pumping of anger and cruelty into the atmosphere. The way to accomplish this is through unconditional love and patience. Watch as the lines of frustration dissipate the next time you greet negativity with compassion. Feel the energy shift from one direction to another. With diligence, we can do this. Love is the last and first piece of the puzzle. With love in our hearts, we come to understand the needs of others. With love, we can transform unnecessary wants into worthwhile needs.

Carry with you always an abundance of patience and understanding, and your plate will never be void of nourishment for others or yourself.

Chapter 10

The Evangelist

*"Do not rely on the outer world as your measuring stick
for your own spiritual growth.
Rely on your response to the outer world
to determine how much you have grown."*
—Bashar

During the winter of 2012, four months after my bike accident, an opportunity to visit a pair of traveling healers presented itself to me through my trusted friend Fiona. My belief in the power of natural healing has been a significant aspect of my core belief system since a very young age. However, I was slightly skeptical, as the pair of healers was of a religious background. As a result of my experience at boarding school, I was aware of the possibility that there is always a chance of encountering misguided intentions; however, at this point in my life, my body was definitely in need of healing through any means possible.

My experiences thus far with religion had not been aligned with my own belief system, yet when I pondered my outcome from private school, it was not all negative. Yes, I was disappointed and angry, among other emotions; but through my strength of will, I did manage to sift out the lessons I was there to learn, even though I was strongly opposed to their methods. Through this process of blocking out one thing and letting another filter through the cheese cloth—skimming the film off the top so to speak—I was able to see clearly certain aspects of life that could serve me well in the future, if I chose that to be so.

While deciding whether to attend this healing session, I concluded that since I was successful in using this method of filtration while attending a stern Christian college, I would surely be able to combat any possible similarities used by these religious healers. Fiona and I decided to give it a shot. The worst thing that could happen would be that we would leave feeling the same way as when we arrived.

Prior to venturing to the miniscule town of Faulkland, BC, I sat quietly and acknowledged the parts of my body that required attention through healing. I had managed to successfully conquer the Lyme disease earlier that year, but the beautiful flora and fauna of my inner rainforest had been the victim of an antibiotic clear cut, so Candida had become my new foe. I have yet to meet a more powerfully willed health enemy as Candida. I asked for healing in this regard while also requesting that my entire body, especially my wrist, gain strength through this evening's process. My body was still recovering from my lack of common sense as I splattered it and my bike across that rock wall.

A channeler had once told me that prior to incarnating into this lifetime, I had chosen to learn my lessons of life the hard way. At the age of forty, I was beginning to understand what that beautiful woman was seeing.

Fiona and I arrived at a church, which was the size of a beaver den, and made our way inside. I grounded myself as we entered

A Soulful Awakening

by envisioning my roots connected to the entire universe, while asking it to assist me in finding healing within through the people inside. The room held about sixty people, and by my estimation, there were about thirty in attendance. The two healers were playing lovely music from a small, elevated stage—he, a Spanish guitar, and she, the organ. My eyes floated toward a djembe, and this made me feel more comfortable as we have one in our home. We slipped into the pew and sat silently, listening to the music before the female healer began to speak.

She introduced herself and her partner as healers appointed by God and informed us that they had been traveling for eight years doing what God had chosen them to do. After her brief introduction, she marched across the floor toward our side of the building. She paused in front of us, raised her arm, and pointed her finger directly at me while intently saying the words, "Tonight, you are going to be healed!" My body began to feel tense, so I reminded myself to relax and be open. I don't know why she singled me out in that moment, as I had never met this woman in my life and my body was free of any noticeable signs of injury. Once she lowered her finger and turned her attention elsewhere, I felt Fiona grab my hand. Part of me felt like bursting out in laughter while another part felt like fleeing from the room. Instead, I chose to be neutral and remained quietly seated.

Her sermon began by informing us of our attachment to evil and if we had any association with practices such as tarot cards, tealeaves, channeling, and so on. She described why these were not Godlike and how they represented the ways of the devil. This particular scene was all too familiar to me. My belief system was under attack once again by organized religion. By this point in my life, I had been to a channeler on three separate occasions, and all three times marked the beginning of significant healing in one way or another. I myself had recently tapped into the non-physical realm through trauma while being forced to sit still to recover. The messages that I had been receiving through this newfound connection had brought significant healing and awareness on a spiritual level to myself, my family and friends, my coworkers, as well as a few strangers, who requested a reading for themselves.

I couldn't relate to this woman, as she implied sternly that channeling and these kinds of connections are evil bearing; this was a contradiction to my own beliefs, which I have developed through experience. I became aware that my body was becoming tense once again, and I felt the beginning stages of anger. I didn't want to blow my chance of being healed and learning through this particular experience, so I began to remind myself of a message that I had recently channeled from a guide. The focus of that lesson was judgment. This has always been a difficult lesson for me and one that I am still far from mastering, but here was a situation that brought with it an opportunity for growth in this capacity.

As she continued to preach, I reminded myself not to judge her for her differences in opinion. If I were to be successful in finding healing through these people, then I would have to try my best to disable my ego from rising. I focused my attention and intention on the healing powers that exist within our world and universe. I focused intently to tap into this while in this room full of fellow travelers of life while focusing attention on the aspects of my physical body that were in need of healing.

My own channeled messages had been a gentle but firm reminder that we are all connected with one another without exception. I had been reminded of the universal truth that we are all on our own journeys, traveling down our own paths while on the same quest. It was my obligation to the collective to except that everyone is learning their own lessons in ways that may differ from mine. I had come to understand that once I chose to look at life through the lens of education, I was better equipped to be open and willing to learn.

As I lost myself in personal affirmations, which I highly suggest doing as often as possible, I realized that she was asking us to raise our hands if we had ever been involved in these metaphysical activities that she was so against. I gently rolled my eyes from side-to-side, attempting to see through my peripheral who was raising their hands; I didn't see any in the air. People were either too intimidated, or I was really the only one who had experiences of these kinds. I thought about leaving my hand down in an attempt to prevent any further attention from being directed at myself, but I heard that little voice inside urging me to be honest. How could I be healed if I were dishonest? That, too, was a contraction to my beliefs, so I slowly raised my hand in pride. I felt like I did at boarding school when I was singled out for being a "bad kid." The healer nodded her head at me and indicated that for now I was off the hook, but I had a distinct feeling that this was not the end of it.

She shifted the direction of her sermon to that of healing, so my comfort level began to increase until I saw someone reaching desperately for my hand as he stretched across the pew in front of me. I felt Fiona jab her finger into my thigh while nodding to my left. There was another man entering our row with his hand out gesturing to me as well. The female healer was addressing the room, "Who is in need of healing tonight?" Buried emotions almost threw my body into the fight-or-flight predicament, so I consciously took myself back to a place of love and trust with the helping wings of the universe. I stood tall and took the man's hand to my left and walked to the front of the room with my head held high and my heart open.

The woman healer had me face the front of the church. Music was playing, and there were two men standing on either side of me with the healer facing the crowd and me. She asked me if I were in need of healing, so I said yes. She then began to chant, and my eyes drifted away from her as I noticed a cow horn that she held in her hands before her. I began to admire its beauty and size as well as the smoothness of its exterior. I took note of the lines that ran so eloquently through it like a road map. I was engulfed in its presence when the sudden movement of the horn itself startled me. The horn then bellowed into my chest with such force that it blew me over. I found myself falling backward. As I began to brace myself, I was caught by the two men who were positioned beside me. They then lowered me gracefully to the floor. The world felt like it was in slow motion as I reluctantly opened my eyelids. The bullhorn was still directed at my chest and was within arm's reach. The healer was standing above me asking God to help her remove the toxicity from my body. At that moment, I believed she meant in a physical sense to promote healing of my physical body, but it soon became clear that she was talking about my channeling abilities and that the devil needed to be removed. I instantly felt the need to ground myself yet again, so as to protect my connections that I felt were under attack. I didn't want these doors to be shut, as they offered valuable wisdom. There was so much energy in the room between the bellowing horn and her beckoning to heal me.

Then I heard her words, "Does anyone smell the sulfur? Do you smell that? That's the devil exiting her body." Indeed I did smell sulfur, but I didn't feel myself transforming from a little red devil. The sulfur episode continued for quite some time, so I took this opportunity to challenge myself to be open to healing while keeping focused attention on my boundaries. At some point, a blanket was draped over my body and I was encouraged to remain on the floor until I was ready to stand up. At first, I was

A Soulful Awakening

apprehensive to open my eyes, so I took a sneak peek. I noticed that the next person was up to bat and I could now remove myself from this playing field when I chose to. The two men who had laid me down were now focused on the woman being currently healed. The churchgoers were watching intently with their hands clasped by their hearts, and the evangelists were doing their job. I couldn't see Fiona, but I was curious to hear what she was thinking. I slowly began to rise with the assistance of a helping hand that graciously returned me to my seat. Fiona seemed speechless, so I whispered to her, "Did she touch me when I fell over?" She said "no" and I said "oh".

I watched others who volunteered to be healed go through a similar process; however, I was the only one who seemed to emit exuberant amounts of sulfur. Eventually, Fiona was pulled to the altar. I watched with the eyes of an eagle hoping not to blink. I didn't want to miss anything; I wanted to see it all from this perspective. The sermon directed toward Fiona began, and then chanting, followed by horn blowing. Fiona then fell backward without a hand being laid on her. The healing process began, as her body lay calm on the floor.

Although Fiona had refrained from raising her hand at the beginning, I knew that she had her own experiences with energy work and channeling, so I was waiting for the sulfur to expel from her body, but she, too, was devil-free. After her healing process, she returned to her seat wrapped in a blanket. She asked me the same question that I had asked her, and my answer was the same. There were no obvious signs of human contact, as we had both fallen backward.

Once everyone in the room had taken their turn, I was pulled back up to the front two more times. Each time I was blown over again and lay on the floor as the healer attempted to remove evil from within me; I didn't smell sulfur these times. I concentrated on asking my non-physical guides for healing and spiritual protection.

The evening concluded, and as Fiona and I drove home, we chalked the night up to another learning experience in life.

I described the event to Steve over coffee the following morning, as the evening was still fresh in my mind. That was an evening I didn't want to forget for so many reasons. After breakfast, we did our morning routine of yoga and exercises. My wrist was still weak from being injured and in a cast for six weeks, so any maneuver that required bearing weight had been painful. As we went through our routine, I found myself in the push-up position numerous times without a huge amount of discomfort. I had been avoiding these postures and exercises until that day. Is it possible that I enabled healing to penetrate on some level that evening?

Through the avenue of intent and awareness, we are able to receive and create healing in a variety of ways. There are synchronistic opportunities that present themselves at all times. It is our choice whether to tap into these occurrences or to ignore them completely. My advice is to utilize all opportunities to the best of our abilities while graciously accepting the lessons in all situations.

Stef: I was at a healing session guided by a religious group last year. I found it difficult to allow myself to be healed while in the process of being judged. Is it possible to find healing under such circumstances?

Solomon: *Healing comes from within. You could find yourself in a position where you are being trampled by a herd of wild animals, and in the moment, even as extreme as it may seem, healing is possible. It is much more difficult, however, because of the forcefulness of energy that you would be experiencing*

A Soulful Awakening

in those moments. The more strenuous the environment is, the more hostile, the more challenging healing becomes. However, it is still possible and within reach at all times. Surrendering to the higher force is imperative. As you surrender to the healing powers of the universe, you instantly let go of doubt, which is critical with any healing. Souls behold the key to healing and life force transformation. Even when you question one's beliefs and someone's own personal reservations, you are capable of receiving healing as long as you, too, let go of judgment.

Remember, life is a reflection. That which we see and question resides strongly within us as well. Without the gift of reflection, it would be difficult to experience that which we like and dislike. Be open and receptive to healing while releasing doubt from the cage of fear, and you will experience the healing you long for.

Chapter 11

We Are All One

"Love and compassion are necessities, not luxuries.
Without them humanity cannot survive."
—Dalai Lama

Stef: Good afternoon, guides and teachers. Could you please remind us of our roots and our collective consciousness?

Coral: *Serenity is the path to travel. Hold serenity in the highest regard. This is a book of truth, just as your life, so share with those you see fit. Encourage spiritual growth in others. We are here to learn and teach collectively from each other. We shall rise above fear and pain. We shall move closer to divinity through diligence and belief. We together are very strong and are gaining strength daily. The movement is very encouraging to all.*

The language of the soul is universal. Peace, love, and compassion do not need passports to cross the borders of society. All they need is intention. From the hills of Somalia to the plains of Pakistan, from the rocky cliffs of Atlantic Canada to the Seven Wonders of the World, to all the wonders left undiscovered. We are all one. Our roots caress each other and share their warmth.

The spiritual well-being of every single cell that inhabits the earth relies on one another, and all have the same origin. The universe is our birthplace; earth is merely a classroom to foster our inner truths. Humanity has seemed to stray from our true understandings, but things are changing. Evolution is underway. These are revolutionary times that we are all a part of. It is really quite magnificent to witness.

Our ultimate achievement is to vibrate on a consistent level continuously and simultaneously with our fellow souls. When our physical bodies are weak and tired, we vibrate on a lower frequency. When we engage in emotional torment, we enable our energy to fluctuate, creating highs and lows. These fluctuations will affect all else, as we are all one.

Hazel: *We are all looking for the same answers to the same questions—questions that flow far beyond life on earth. We were not put here on earth; we chose to be here. We did not choose to be slaves to money; we did not choose to be slaves to greed, power, and ego. We did not choose to be representatives of fear and anger. These are born as a by-product of misrepresentation of our purpose on this planet.*

The road to recovery is being paved, and it is time to choose a new course. If we choose this course as one, as a whole, collectively, the road will widen and breach the banks of uncertainty. As a group, we will follow the ways of the wolf. The wolf travels as a pack, as this enables the entirety of the group to reach their destination safely and soundly. The pack shares wisdom, virtues, guidance, lessons learned, and lessons to be discovered and create harmony along the way.

Fear on the planet is reaching heights unknown, but love for all will burst the bubble of this imaginary entity.

Grandpa Harold: *Always keep in mind what is most important. Love for all those around you. Love for not only those that you are close to, but also those with whom you would not normally meet on a personal basis. If your intentions are based on love, all else will fall into place.*

The magic of mysticism surrounds the very core of who we are. Without mystery, we are no more. We are all equal with needs to be addressed in the hope of reaching a place of completeness as one. We have always been one, will continue to be one, and will work together as one.

The universe calls out to all those souls who have the strength, courage, patience, resilience, and faith to set all courses straight. As you can see, the physical world around you is falling apart at the seams; but together with intent, all this will change. Times of greed and hate will dissipate. Gather in groups to foster the truth.

A fine sprinkle of love left behind will eventually cover up hate completely. Navigate with the upmost respect for both yourself and your fellow souls, who are simply extensions of your own soul. Do this today, tomorrow, and every day that follows, and you will experience love and respect in a whole new light. Love the man who unknowingly bumps you in the grocery store the same as you would love the soul who greets you with a hug. This is true compassion and love for one another.

You are loved even when love feels like it does not exist. There is love all around you. Each breath you take is a direct line to the roots of all souls. Without love, this line of continual exchange of energy would not exist. When in doubt, take a deep breath and feel what you breathe. It is not just air that fills our lungs—it is love that fills our hearts, which in turn brings new life to our souls.

Stef: Last night, I felt embarrassed by the negativity that I experienced by another. I have been trying to tell myself that we are all on our own path working in conjunction with one another, but there are times when I allow the actions of others to bother me. How best do we handle these moments in time?

Ruby: *Let them pass through you unobstructed. Do what you can to bring forth awareness in the moment, expel positive energy, and ask the universe to grant every soul with compassion and understanding for one another. Refrain from judgment in any form.*

These reactions that humans engage in are simply bad habits. They give a false sense of control and power. These are things that should not exist in a perfect world, but they are very real in your days. Part of the human lesson is to manage these situations as best as you are able. It takes courage and strength to speak outwardly, especially to strangers, but this is part of your journey. Live by example and speak through your soul. Reach within to find the appropriate words for lessons to be shared. Not everyone will grasp or care to grasp what you attempt to pass on, but that is okay. You will have planted a seed, which will be watered at some point in time. You will have done your share, and this will bring you contentment and peace both within your heart and mind.

Remember that there is strength in groups. Companions of spiritual growth increase our momentum, and the vortex will become wider and more effective. Feel the energy of all those around you as you carry on your journeys as one. Surround yourself with compassion and peaceful warriors of the universe; together you will harvest the fruits that you have sown as a whole. There is huge potential in working coherently as a group in gatherings. Sharing, experiencing, learning, teaching, and simply caring for each other will bring peace globally and universally.

Stephanie Banks

The world around you is expanding and contracting like never before. The deeper you breathe, the deeper the entire world will breathe. Each breath inhaled and each breath exhaled contributes to the universal breath of fostering healing and love within all.

Stef: The sun is shining and the temperature is warm. I feel frustrated and irritated, not to mention disappointed with our son's behavior lately. There are times when he acts ungrateful even though he doesn't need anything else in his life. He eats well and has a warm and loving home and clean water to drink and wash with. He participates in activities and has the required gear needed. Does anyone have any words of wisdom for all of us who are struggling with similar situations?

Solomon: *We all learn, and we all have a universal responsibility to teach. Sometimes we are the students, and other times we are the instructor. Sometimes we are both simultaneously. Both roles serve a purpose to ourselves and others but are of equal importance.*

When we are not in need of anything, we do not understand the feeling of being in need. Our bellies must grumble before we conceptualize the pain of being hungry. Our feet must ache before we truly appreciate the comfort of soft souls. Our skin must burn before we appreciate the shade that provides us shelter. Many children in your society have not experienced these things; however, as you know, there are many places worldwide where children do suffer from the lack of certain requirements of the physical and emotional body.

Children of the privileged type need to look into the eyes of the suffering children before enlightenment of this description will truly transpire. If traveling to see those eyes is not feasible, much can be experienced through videos and photographs. It is up to the world to deliver these messages to children who need not, and it is up to these children to expand their depth of compassion. Remind your children that we are all one.

Stef: Good afternoon, guides, teachers, and protectors. Would you be so kind as to give us a few words on our connection to each other?

Raphael: *On occasion, fear raises its ugly face. You must dig deep into your emotional toolbox to understand that fear is not nearly as powerful as we allow it to be from time to time. Let go of what once was; do not think about what will be. Live only for this moment—this precious moment in time. Each moment is one step closer to eternity. Ask us to envelope you in our curtain of understanding and unconditional love. Through pain comes understanding. The key is to let go of hurt and confusion, circumstances just are. They come and go just as the sun and rain. The realization that life sometimes brings forth judgment, hurt, and anger eventually allows us to recognize nonjudgment, love, happiness, contentment, and peace. Look deep within your heart for the love that exists and focus your attention on that feeling. Love thyself, and be patient with thyself.*

Look to the sun and stars when dark times come upon you, and brilliance will shine through the clouds and radiate joy through your physical body and penetrate your spirit. Travel together in groups of love—flocks of emanating love and wisdom. Through diligence you will achieve great enlightenment and will share what you have learned with complete faith and harmony.

Open your heart completely without judgment or expectations. Trust in love and your need to find true happiness and peace. Find others that will be receptive and encouraging to your spiritual growth. Open your heart and soul completely to the energy that surrounds you.

Your experiences will differ from others, but that is how it should be. We are all traveling down our own path, but our destination is always the same. We walk with our own stride, march to our own beat, pause for our own duration, but must have respect for one another's journey as we travel through this plane as one. Our roots are all connected to the same origin but must find their own way to the fountain of everlasting love.

Let go of your insecurities as they serve society, not your soul. Set your intentions daily, and keep them simple and clear, precise, and to the point. Respect your emotions as you experience them throughout your days but strive for uniformity in your heart. If allowed to roam free, emotions will suffocate your spirit and create chaos in an otherwise stable environment. Remember to use the sun to exchange negative and toxic energy for new, positive energy. The sun is our route to warmth and understanding, to serenity and calmness. Even when the sun does not shine, the pathway is clear.

Find solace within yourself and those around you. Reach out to those in need with a simple smile or touch. Feel love spread throughout the universe as we converse with one another in this fashion.

Stef: Could you please tell me about yourself?

Raphael: *I live in your heart. I pump your blood when needed. I am able to remove toxins. I am a conductor of electromagnetic energy, which, if used properly, is capable of snuffing out toxic waste as it builds within human bodies, affecting our spiritual connection. When meditating, ask for me to cleanse your bodies* and illuminate goodness. I am a protector of the spirit from emotional damage, but as always, this requires intent from the beholder, the bearer of toxicity.

Stef: Were you ever on the plane of earth?

Raphael: *Yes, I was. I was a king—ruler of many in one lifetime. I had control at my fingertips but did not allow power to elude my vision. I was a peaceful warrior who recognized the importance of collective consciousness. Together we are stronger, and together we create many wonderful outcomes. My queen was from Persia. We did not foster negative feelings or secrets. We taught but never fought. We shared, but our emotions never flared. We were one but individually bound to our own direction and course. Our sails blew in the same manner but were separate from one another. We had a son who died at a young age; we allowed his soul to pass as it had chosen to do.*

Sherman H. Harlow: *Look for the bigger picture of how souls are interconnected and woven together so intricately. Glide eloquently through time with regard for everything. Caress each other through thought and daily intent. Warm each other's souls simply by applying love and devotion through your energy. This flow of love will be unobstructed by mountains or buildings. It will be unstoppable, as long as we ask it to flow freely and continuously.*

Love with life in your heart. Live with love in your life.

I love you all and live with you daily.

Chapter 12

Times Are Changing

"Abundance is
the ability to do what you need to do
when you need to do it."
—Bashar

Stef: Good morning to all our guides, teachers, and protectors. Ustro mentioned to me that we are in the heat of powerful times, a spiritual movement of sorts. I have since read various other authors who also speak of this. Can anyone elaborate on these changing times?

Solomon: *Times are changing. Things are beginning to shift. Movements of all sorts are underway. Some are natural, and some are not. Nature will always prevail even when it seems like a losing battle. The authentic power of the people is very influential. We can move rocks the size of mountains merely by using awareness and intention.*

Fear can dominate all other emotions if left to breed. We are seeing a strong awakening and remember how humans tend to learn. You have heard the expression, "Hitting rock bottom." This term can apply to your current era. The human race has lost sight, but the universe is compassionate and patient. The wheels are in motion. Do not make decisions based on fear, because those decisions only reflect our intellect, not our spirituality.

Understand that the way the world operates currently is outdated, past its prime, expired. What do you do with your expired yogurt? You keep it awhile longer in your fridge for no particular reason until it grows moldy and toxic, at which time you realize that that yogurt that started out as a beautiful culture has been neglected and that which once served a beneficial purpose must be discarded and replaced with new. Our ways, our traditional ways, are still retrievable as long as we are successful in skimming off the top layer of film and stirring the pot, so to speak.

Engage in what you are drawn to. March to the rhythm of your own soul, value the opinions of others, but remember your path is directed only by your own intuition—no one else's. Plan not to react. Bear in mind that you are on a journey to learn, teach, care, and nurture. If you follow these steps in accordance with the lessons of self-love, you will find peace. This awareness is awakening and re-emerging in many during this time. Feel it and live it, as it is all that is.

Stef: Good evening, universe and all that transpires within it. We have been discussing the changing times within our world. Does anyone have a message that they would like to share with us today?

Sherman H. Harlow: *The seasons are shifting, as is the universal consciousness. The light within human kind has been switched on, and many will be seeking answers to questions that they ponder daily. The collectiveness of all is moving in a direction of higher learning and understanding.*

Stephanie Banks

These times have been created by all souls, and simultaneously we embark on this journey of learning about our true nature. Our true nature is growth in a soulful sense as opposed to a material sense. This material importance is becoming mundane and boring to many, and therefore, it is dissipating while making way for more valuable belief systems and priorities. As we reprioritize and reorganize our lives to allow room for spiritual growth, we will become more energized and feel vitalized. This feeling will be a pleasant and a welcome change for many. Life is in an upward motion, not just for those within arm's reach, but for all souls within the universe. Guide each other through compassion, patience, and understanding.

The state of the world's economics is reflective of the state of our spiritual well-being as a whole. Humanity has strayed too far from the ground in which our roots reside. There are many souls that have yet to feel and experience dirt between their toes. The soil is our source of grounding and our place of connection and conductivity of spiritual refinement. Remove your rubber soles and place your feet in the dirt. As you experience this feeling of connectedness to your source, remind your mind of your purpose for being here. Is your purpose here to consume, destroy, and continuously build upon your acquisitions of material goods and useless commodities that add to the global economy of greed and narcissism?

This is not your purpose, nor is it the purpose of your fellow souls. Your purpose is far more meaningful and exemplary of human interaction with all living creatures. Economics disables the natural harmonious way of being simply by existing. Economics are a by-product of the ego, which has been allowed to transform into power and greed. The division that has developed as a result of this misused power has become too great, and the authentic power within us all has stepped in with the intent to rectify an unstable and unsustainable societal clause known to man as money.

The current economic state worldwide is showing signs of crumbling and dismantling. Do not be afraid of this transition; remember resilience as you feel this new beginning. With dedication to all life, we will reach a place of universal understanding. Our misguided thoughts have led us to the dependency of money for our survival, but this illusion has reached a dead end. We must find an alternate route as we return to source. We are source.

Money is not and will never be our savior. Love is our true path of finding our road to recovery. We have a long road ahead of us on this journey, but it is necessary for this evolution to evolve fully and completely. The removal of economics will bring fully enlightened liberation to all. When the currency of self-improvement in a materialistic sense is demobilized, we will return to our true currency of universal self-representation as a whole.

We are here to grow and prosper alongside all life in unison, not in opposition. If humanity continues to be opposed, the battle for essential needs and nonessential things will destroy what we are actually all about, which is to find peace and tranquility in all avenues of ourselves. Our own roots are the avenues to all other roots. If we sever our roots from the roots of all other natural living souls, we are severing our own breath.

The group: *Simply apply and share the principles that are being introduced to you and you will begin to live in a reality that accepts and promotes change within your space and time on earth. Wander down this road of love and compassion, seeking clarity and brilliance.*

Brilliance *is a word that needs to be rediscovered. Brilliance can be seen from all realms and grows in leaps and bounds simply by acknowledging its presence. Brilliance is eternal energy in its finest, purest form. It is energy undirected by human intervention. It is light undisturbed. It is white and magical. It does not have matter but does matter. The energetic force of brilliance surrounds our spirits and magnifies universal wisdom. How do we achieve brilliance? With focused attention on all that symbolizes the heart, compassion, understanding, empathy, and clarity of the spiritual realm.*

Focus your thoughts and understand the gift of the words left unspoken. Feel the currents of freedom rush through your physical body and out through your soul. We are capable of bearing witness to all dimensions if only we believe—believe in ourselves, believe in others and the belief in the truth that reflects the building blocks of the universe. Ancient civilizations have built their temples one block at a time, and with one foul swoop, those temples can be dismantled but never destroyed.

We are here to create and to imagine the possibilities that lay before us. We as humans have created beautiful tools in which to draw from. These tools assist in our teachings and understandings. Find the tools that suit your needs, and implement them in ways that you see fit. For some, it may be writing; for others, it may be creating beautiful images. For others, it may be conquering a magnificent mountaintop. The tools for self-discovery are endless and at our disposal.

Acknowledge how your thoughts come to you. Although thoughts are of the mind, they are imperative to our growth. New ways of thinking will need to take place. Think of this as a lesson in creative thought. The use of color in thought is a very wonderful and powerful tool. Words can be replaced or summarized by using colors. Some colors are calming and healing; some are energizing; and others evoke a sense of pain or despair.

Understanding the use of colors will bring you closer to energy, and in turn, closer to the universal laws and our own souls. Shapes, geometry, and symbols are also great tools for understanding, learning, and healing. All three have been used without failure throughout the ages. Energy is able to take on any shape at any time. Symbols bring forth awareness; learn to recognize their meanings. By simply focusing our attention on a symbol or a shape, we are able to develop an intention. With intention we form an outcome.

Listen, remember, realize, dream, and wonder. Use your imagination and the tools that have been created for you by others who are simply extensions of yourselves, as you recognize that times are changing.

Conclusion

"You only have control over three things in life.
The thoughts you think, the images you
visualize, and the actions you take.
How you use these three things determines
everything you experience.
If you don't like what you're producing and experiencing,
you have to change your responses."
—Jack Cranfield

In August of 2012, my body hurdled through the air, attached to a mountain bike with both my son and life partner in the background watching as I planted a full-body kiss onto a rock face. The imprint of that rock has been engraved in the memory bank of my life. This book is a testament to the silver lining that exists in every situation. There is always a happy note to be played as long as we are open to all possibilities at all times and focus our entire self on being still just long enough to create a positive outcome.

Simply through our thoughts, we become the creators of our own masterpiece, the artist of our lifetimes. The only limitations that truly exist are creations of our own. We manifest and illuminate our course as we so choose. As we open our eyes, both externally and internally, we begin to see clearly the view that we would like to manifest moment to moment. For me, this view was blurry, but now the clouds are beginning to part as they make way for new light to shine. The clouds will never truly disappear, as I will need them to water my seeds from time to time. These clouds act as a constant reminder that dark times do exist, but it's up to us to overcome these troubling moments.

The universe has become my partner in daily energy exchange; I encourage all of you to do the same. Simply close your eyes, breathe deeply, and envision the universe removing all the negative energy that has accumulated throughout the day. As you do this, allow yourself to receive renewed, positive energy that flows freely when we ask it to. Once you feel that your energy field has been replenished, I encourage you to set your intentions through visualization. Ask for patience for yourself and others; ask to remember gratitude as you travel through another day. Ask that you be accepting of yourself and all others. Take this time to set any intentions that you feel will contribute to the creation of peaceful moments and watch how your days unfold. This is so simple yet remarkably impactful.

The universe is comprised of many realms and realities, but the universal truths are the same within all. These lessons are presented to you as gifts for you to explore as you wish. You may choose to close this book and continue to live as you have been without exploring these ideas any further, and that's okay. You are living in accordance with your own compass set in your own direction at your own pace. On the other hand, you may decide to delve into your inner self and seek the answers you are looking for. When the reading of these pages is complete, you may decide to look at everything just a little differently and acknowledge the beauty that you create by simply living with love in your heart.

The choice is yours, as we are the masters of our design, the architect of our pillar. Is your pillar being held together precariously with fear and doubt? If so, challenge yourself to remove the bricks one at a time, give them a scrub, and begin to build a new foundation based on trust, faith, understanding, love, compassion, acceptance, and freedom. Take as much time as you need to do this; time is replenished as long as it is not wasted.

For some, the idea of universal guides, teachers, protectors, and spirit animals from other realms within ours is an idea that will not resonate; and for others, this concept will not be new. It doesn't matter how you decide to read these teachings. What matters is that you read them and contemplate their meanings.

I feel incredibly grateful to have the opportunity to pass these ancient words of understanding on to all those who are willing to open themselves to a way of life that will create harmony on all levels. When we learn to cohabitate in harmony with all souls at all times, we experience peace as a whole, as one.

We are one; our roots tap into the same source and drink from the same fountain. As you expand your horizons and create your new landscape of love, remember to have fun, relax, and enjoy. Do not be afraid; be excited!

Stef: We have come to the conclusion of this book, and with a heart full of love, we say thank you for all the wonderful, magical, life-transforming words of wisdom. Sherman, would you like to conclude our thoughts?

Sherman H. Harlow: *When we walk with truth in our hearts, we are able to let go of the anchor that binds our souls. Our souls are meant to be free—free to roam and explore. They are meant to be weightless and energetic. When we as humans are fearful of the unknown, we anchor ourselves to an emotion that debilitates our spirit and our physical self. By placing complete faith in ourselves, those we trust on earth, and our universe, we enable our souls to roam as they please, which is with ease.*

Allow for new doors to open as others close. Look for opportunities to present themselves to you in unconventional ways. There is so much more to experience. Refrain from spinning without a destination. Seek clarity within your heart. Within your heart resides your innermost desires and ambitions. Create new boundaries for yourself, as your current ones may have expired. Relinquish thought processes that are not your own that you have adopted along the way. To see your heart clearly, you must remove all thoughts completely and feel your inner self.

Connect yourself through vision and intentions to all the souls. Caress and nurture your spirit, as this is truly what it needs. It is difficult at times, of course, but believe in your intuition, your strength, your courage, your patience, and your determination. Follow your own yellow brick road to clarity. Return to your roots that are intertwined with the rest of the world and universe. Draw from this endless, vast source of energy and wisdom as needed. It is there for all to drink from and contribute to.

Become a contributor rather than merely a consumer. Find your passion and embark on your life here with full attention on your inner self and the non-physical world that resides all around you. Walk your road while savoring every step. This is your creation, so create your own beautiful play of happiness.

Rise and fall as all of us shall
but always return to your roots that run deep
They are embedded in time for all to remember and share
As you nourish your roots, ask for the truth

to set you free of restless unruth
Ruthless lives are living with ties
that bind their souls to dead-end skies
As the clouds begin to part
Warmth will set you apart
From the shackled souls of unloving roles
The time is here again, as a new day has begun
To play the part of an unfailing heart
There is order and peace in universal beliefs
That strengthens with efforts of followers of calm
Your faith is strong, your legacy to live on
Empower yourself and those you seek
To share the magic of a world not so bleak

Believe, my friends, in the wonders of the worlds floating around yours, encircling, rotating, and obligating all to continually stand tall.

Affirmations and Poems

"Raise your words, not your voice.
It is rain that grows flowers, not thunder."
—Rumi

Unveiling Buried Emotions
I hereby stand before my buried emotions with enthusiasm
To deliver them to a higher understanding
I intend to reveal my past to myself through love and compassion
I will not judge others nor myself
As I process my feelings and acknowledge their existence
I will allow myself the freedom to laugh, cry, or scream where needed
I will not enable my emotions to bring physical or emotional harm
To either others or myself
Once I have acknowledged each emotion that lies beneath my veil of uncertainty
I will ask the universe to grant me the strength and trust
To release it back to the universe forever
        -Ustro

Standing Tall
Good morning, world shining bright
In the midst of delight

Share with me still
If you make it your will
I will listen and learn
Throughout every twist and turn
I am here for all
I will stand tall
I will forever believe and foster my faith
As all that you share continues to unlace
I ask for compassion to follow my passion
Of forever caring and wisdom bearing
            -Stef

Daily Affirmation
Live without judgment
Breathe with intention
Speak with direction
Sleep in peace
Listen with compassion
Pray without expectation
            -Solomon

Trust
I believe in myself and my intuition wholly and completely
The universe is my guide, teacher, and protector
The sun is my savior
            -Solomon

Enlightenment
As I gaze into the distant skies
I see not only the vision through my eyes
I see twinkling here and there
I see enlightenment everywhere
I see it as the magical reincarnation of all that we are
I see it as the light between the moon and that star

Forever feel enlightenment through peace and calm
Feel it from eve through 'til dawn
      -Solomon

Return to your Roots
Rise and fall, as all of us shall, but always return to your roots that run deep
They are embedded in time for all to remember and share
As you nourish your roots, ask for the truth to set you free of restless unruth
Ruthless lives are living with ties that bind their souls to dead-end skies
As the clouds begin to part
Warmth will set you apart
From the shackled souls of unloving roles
The time is here again as a new day has begun
To play the part of an unfailing heart
There is order and peace in universal beliefs
That strengthens with efforts of followers of calm
Your faith is strong, your legacy to live on
Empower yourself and those you seek
To share the magic of a world not so bleak
      -Sherman H. Harlow

Staying True
Do not wallow
Wallowing is for hippos
Do not fret
Fretting is a waste of energy
Ask for courage to stand tall
Ask for compassion within all
Look for the light that shines bright
In your soul and the collective whole
Dig deep to find your strength

This will keep you at arm's length
Of the harsh and cruel deeds
Of other's rotten seeds
Allow words of unkindness to pass through your being
Through to a world of spiritual seeing
Remind yourself of your gifts, which are many
These cannot be taken away, unless you give them that way
Hold them tight to your heart as you wake to a new start
In the day that now begins with love, laughter, and peace
      -Sherman H. Harlow

The Evolving Soul
Let it be known
Let it all be shown
The ways, the worlds, the ever-changing lives that we seek
We walk, we talk, we idle, we run
As fast and as slow as only we will allow ourselves to go
We watch, we listen, we see, and we hear
But forever follow in the footsteps of fear
Relinquish this habit and set it free
For there is so much more for you to be
      -Sherman H. Harlow

Our Curtain Call
Look for change within
As a new day will always begin
Drop that dime and watch it as it falls
Through the cracks of those concrete walls
Of fame and fortune that will not withstand the call
Of wisdom from within to aid and care for your fellow souls
Who lie between those cracks in sunken holes
Reach for the hands that struggle to find fresh air and bright light
That lead to a safe zone from emotional blight
This is a human right

The world is hungry for unconditional love
Free from the glove that strangles the soul
Release the grasp of consumption
Without the assumption
That the world will falter, minus this thing called money
Taste the sweetness of the honey that flows from the hive
Of compassion, love, and understanding
That reminds us of all that we require to thrive
Be at one with yourselves
Be at one with all, as this is our curtain call—to make way for change
　　-Sherman H. Harlow

Childs Affirmation
I am beautiful
I am smart
I am very kind
I am full of love
I will not judge others
I am happy in my heart
I will always do my best
　　-Hazel

The Time Piece
Time is a healer
Time is precious
Time is universal
Time is necessary
Time never stops
Time is fundamental
Time creates new beginnings continually
There are no ends
　　-Hazel

Channeled Definitions

"I would rather attempt to do something and fail
than attempt to do nothing and succeed."
—Robert H. Schuller

Unruth: *an ancient term used to reference unrest, lack of peace and calmness. When tranquility and equilibrium of mind and soul is lacking, so, too, is love and compassion. When one lacks love and compassion, reactions to circumstances take place. Reactions can lead to many outcomes, many of which reflect negative emotions. To be ruthless means to be unforgiving under all circumstances.*

Coherence: *the union between beings that peacefully includes all reflection of those beings. We all have refined needs physically, emotionally, and spiritually. Coherence arrives when respect for all is present. Coherence is born when all those involved reach a selfless realm, mutually cohabitating with one another while being accepting of each other on all levels.*

Diligence: *the understanding that with perseverance you will achieve your goals. It means mustering all that you have within both your physical body and your higher intuitive self to find a way to be successful in your quest, whatever that may be. It* means looking at the obstacles that lie in your path as merely a contribution to your building blocks of life. It means always having faith in yourself, those you trust, your alternate realities, and your journey. It means envisioning the desired outcome for which you are yearning for. It is knowing deep within you that you are strong, capable, willing, and have the desire to achieve what you set out to do with respect and love for all those with whom you meet along your way.

Virtue: *truth uncovered. It is what lies beneath the rubble. Virtue is the underlying values within one's soul. To find virtue, one must look far beyond the obvious state of affairs. Virtue is true understanding of any situation. Virtue requires respect for oneself and others. With virtue comes trust and faith. Virtue is relative regard for all that we know and understand. To have virtue means to live with integrity. Virtue is the understanding of what is right and what is not. It is the compilation of all that we know of a subject and interpreting it, as it should be.*

Harmony: *the understanding of the needs of others and ourselves. It requires being compassionate of those needs and working together to achieve those needs so as to create a stable environment for all.*

Equilibrium: *equal-I-am. Equality at its finest. All beings symbolized by each other as being the same. Neither being worse nor better than the other. When two or more states become truly equal, equilibrium follows suit. To maintain this state of equality, we must achieve equilibrium. Better yet, when a state of equality has been reached, equilibrium is the state of maintaining this balance of equality.*

Karma: *the give-and-take analogy in a universal sense. We have designed our lives in such a way that everything we say and do* will have a cause and an effect. Feed the poor, and you, too, shall be fed. Be trustworthy, and you to will experience trust in others. Pick up that homeless piece of trash, and your own yard will be clean. For some, karma has been designed to come into effect instantaneously, and for others, it may take a lifetime or many lifetimes before the full effect takes its full course. There is no need to be fearful of karma, as many are, because it's our ally. Karma is our guiding light at the end of a dark tunnel. Without karma to keep us moving in the direction of ascension, the world would spin in chaos. This is simply unorderly and not at all how our universe operates. There is order and structure as you have been experiencing. As your soul evolves, karma becomes more of a driving force within your life. Some lessons are learned the hard way, and others come quite easily; our path determines this. Karma is universal but distinct to each individual in each circumstance. Ask karma to stand close by, and you will learn your lessons without karma actually entering your kingdom. Acknowledge your right to be your own karmic ruler. Karma will come regardless, but it is always more pleasant to be the keeper of your own palace.

Reality: *for the most part, reality is a false perception of time and space. It has become one-dimensional and blurred. One's true reality is unobstructed by chaotic nonsense. It is an inside view of the non-physical world, where great learning and creativity transpires. It is where harmony exists among the souls of the universe. Earthy reality is dictated by money, greed, and power struggles. When one looks at the animal kingdom, it becomes evident that money, greed, and power are unnecessary in creating harmonious living.*

Enlightenment: *it is magic, it is pure, it is divine, it is truth. It is an opening to a new beginning. The click before we speak. The crack in the door before it becomes ajar. Enlightenment is a route unto* its own. A road less traveled, yet one that needs to be explored. It is a twinkle of an eye, a momentary glimpse of something so real and pure. Do not blink in this moment, capture all that you are able, and imprint this moment in your soul to be forever there.

Reconciliation: *the event that takes place when one comes to terms with an action that is typically unsatisfactory in regards to spiritual growth. It is the understanding of circumstances that lead to choices of inadequacy. It is the acceptance of those choices followed by new choices made in order for the soul to feel at peace.*

Clarity: *the realization of simplicity. Simplify each moment of being alive; boil it down to the nakedness of truth. Truth being love and compassion for all that exists. Clarity is the moment we see without opening our eyes. It is the vision of realms that exist well beyond the outer limits of our minds and atmosphere. Clarity is a moment of magic that creates a beautiful image that will never be replaced or damaged. Clarity amplifies all that we know of our inner selves, our higher being, and the insight that we allow to be our driving force through the highway of enlightenment.*

Love: *emanates, illuminates, and penetrates our core when barriers that block it are dissolved. Love is an unconditional feeling of pure gratitude and acceptance of another soul. It represents purity of our own soul residing in union with the purity of another soul.*

Equanimity: *the true understanding of self. It is your raw, natural state of being unobstructed by wants, desires, struggles, satisfaction, dissatisfaction, emotional responses, or reactions. It is a clear view of who you really are once all of whom you have become is set aside. It is your true reflection, your soul exposed. To become truly soulful means finding equanimity within, which* takes time and patience. Once all souls find equanimity of self simultaneously, they will reach universal equilibrium. A master plan achieved.

Ingenuity: the art of adaptation. It is the ability to create in a hostile environment. It means looking at a situation as a welcome challenge with a positive outcome rather than an impossible task not worth expelling energy into. Ingenuity is the refinement of one's skills and the development of new ones with the intent to maneuver around obstacles that are in your way of achieving your goals. It is a sister to resilience. They walk hand-in-hand.

Brood: brood not, and you shall find inner peace within all situations. Brooding is a glorified way of describing worry. To brood means to overanalyze a situation, which will always lead to confusion, debilitation, and obstruction of true, unrestricted reality in a universal sense. Karmic response means to do the right thing for the correct purpose while accepting the responsibility to avoid questioning the outcome. Once we learn to continuously base our responses and actions on a karmic plane naturally without thought of why, we will be able to effectively remove brooding from our lives. Brooding results in internal manipulation and anguish as we question circumstances. As long as actions are taken as a result of our inner light guiding us, there will be no need for afterthought or deliberation. Brooding and worry create havoc emotionally, which will inevitably lead to physical breakdowns within the body.

Transmitter: accumulates information from another source and accurately transfers that information to another source. Imprinting an idea from one to another. To transmit means to describe, in understood terminology, a concept that is not your own, a concept from one that needs to be relayed to another through a source. The transmitter is in an unbiased position. Neutral.

The transmitter may very well have an opinion but refrains from expressing that opinion as to allow the receiver to form their own beliefs based on the details being transmitted as accurately as possible. The stronger the connection that the transmitter has to the source, the more accurate the transmission will be. There is a difference between transmission and translation. A transmission does not lose touch with the origin of the source; a translation is an account of information that was transmitted at one point but may have been manipulated by another. It is impossible to avoid translation, because the moment that ideas are shared is the moment when the transmission ends. Transmission of thoughts, concepts, and ideas can only be transmitted from the source to another once. After this moment in time, those concepts become open for discussion and, in turn, translation.

Congruency: *represents alignment of all. It is the assimilation of ideas and wisdom that will then allow the beholder to find equanimity of mind, body, and soul. Congruent means to see on a level plane. Congruency is when thoughts and behavior patterns are not in conflict with one another. It is to have achieved a balance between thought and intuition. To have acquired an even playing field within one self on a spiritual level while living in harmony with other souls. Congruency is to maintain a constant state of understanding of both one's self and others. To maintain congruency is to exist in a parallel relationship with all other souls who are moving toward the same destination of compassion, love, and understanding; parallel lines within the universe.*

About the Author

Stephanie Banks is an award-winning author who is quickly making her mark as an accomplished author. She was born into a family of intuitives who encouraged fostering faith in accepting guidance from within as well as from other realms that surround our own. Prior to Stephanie's near-death experience she led a life directed by modern day terms that lacked depth and clarity. Immediately following her encounter with death her life transformed to that of an awakened soul. She has now dedicated her life to mastering ancient wisdom and writing candidly about all that she learns through this process. Her unfailing connection to the non-physical realm has offered guidance and transformation to all those that seek profound insight into our existence.

Stephanie, attended the University of Western Ontario and is currently enrolled in the master class of spiritual enlightenment. She lives with her family in British Columbia Canada.

CPSIA information can be obtained at www.ICGtesting.com
Printed in the USA
LVOW06s0340051114

411831LV00001B/19/P